DISCAR

ROMAN HOUSE CHURCHES FOR TODAᵢ

ROMAN HOUSE CHURCHES FOR TODAY

A Practical Guide for Small Groups

Reta Halteman Finger

WILLIAM B. EERDMANS PUBLISHING COMPANY

GRAND RAPIDS, MICHIGAN / CAMBRIDGE, U.K.

First edition © 1993 Herald Press
Second edition © 2007 Reta Halteman Finger

This edition published 2007 by
Wm. B. Eerdmans Publishing Co.
2140 Oak Industrial Drive N.E., Grand Rapids, Michigan 49505 /
P.O. Box 163, Cambridge CB3 9PU U.K.
www.eerdmans.com

Printed in the United States of America

11 10 09 08 07   7 6 5 4 3 2 1

Library of Congress Cataloging-in-Publication Data

Finger, Reta Halteman, 1940-
    Roman house churches for today: a practical guide for small groups /
    Reta Halteman Finger. — 2nd ed.
        p.   cm.
    Rev. ed. of: Paul and the Roman house churches, c1993.
    Includes bibliographical references and index.
        ISBN 978-0-8028-0764-9 (pbk.: alk. paper)
    1. Bible. N.T. Romans — Study and teaching — Simulation methods.
    2. Bible. N.T. Romans — Social scientific criticism. 3. House churches — Italy —
    Rome.   I. Finger, Reta Halteman, 1940- Paul and the Roman house churches.   II. Title.

BS2665.55.F56   2007
227'.1007 — dc22

                                                            2007027527

For resources to use with this book, go to
http://www.nbts.edu/academics/faculty/wiles/romans/simul.htm

To my parents,

    Wilmer M. Halteman and

        Perle Guntz Halteman (1918-2003), who

            first taught me to appreciate

                and enjoy the Bible

Contents

Foreword

In my seminary classes I often find laypersons who will remain laypersons but are hungry to study the Bible and questions of faith in the same rigorous ways by which they stay current in their jobs and other interests. They want to know what current scholarship offers and to tackle life-and-death questions of meaning and wholeness.

They believe — rightly! — that such teaching and learning should be taking place in their own faith communities. This book provides opportunities for any church that cares about building community, working toward justice, and involving older youth and adults in Bible study that can transform individuals and the faith community. I am enthusiastic about inviting you to engage in this simulation study of Paul's epistle to the Romans.

"It's amazing! fun! hard work!" "How could I ever have read Romans as 'dry doctrine' when it is alive and invites me into a world I need to know if I am to understand God's Word to me today?" You will hear such comments if you follow Reta Finger into the Rome of Paul's day. Her book offers tools you need to *experience* the Bible in life-changing ways. Such study is risky because it invites us to hear Paul's letter to the Romans as it was first heard by slaves and free, women and men, poor and rich; and then to hear it today as the people of God in our setting. When we "have ears to hear," we will be led to grow and change.

This resource takes Scripture so seriously that we find ourselves struggling to grasp every word. It places these words in their sociopolitical context so we can sense what they meant to Prisca and Mary, Tryphaena and Persis, Aquila and Apellus. Knowing something about their situations, we begin to hear the words with them. Once we have encountered Paul's words through their senses, we can apply them in fresh ways for ourselves.

Teaching through simulation is *hard work*. It requires teachers to prepare well; students also must be willing to invest in the process. But like simulations we do inter-generationally or with children (as in *Marketplace, 29 A.D.*), most find that the investment is well worth the effort.

This book is designed to draw learners into the biblical text and the first-century context. What was life like in Rome? for Jews? for women? for slaves? for the well-to-do? for those free but poor? for Christians in households where the head of the household was not Christian? Through action and reflection, learners become first-century persons in Rome and then step outside that world to reflect in our own time and place. Thus we hear and understand the text in new and powerful ways today.

Finger summarizes contemporary New Testament scholarship in ways that make it accessible and relevant. The helpful suggestions on how to set up and lead the simulation are invaluable. What it requires is this: a teacher or team of teachers willing to learn through class preparation; commitment by group members to attend regularly for ten to twelve weeks; willingness to engage the text and other group members in honest and forthright ways; and expectancy that God's Word may touch us in life-changing ways.

You will discover: that laypersons can handle Scripture study that makes use of biblical scholarship; challenge and reward; new insights into Paul's letter to the church at Rome; new ways to access all the epistles and the Bible in general; a growing appreciation for what it means to say the Bible is "a living book"; and a clearer sense of who God is calling you to be and what God is calling you to do.

LINDA J. VOGEL
Senior Scholar
Garrett-Evangelical Theological Seminary
Evanston, Illinois

Preface

In the fall of 1987, I began a year of course work at Garrett-Evangelical Theological Seminary in Evanston, Illinois. My area of interest was New Testament, and the only course on a New Testament document offered that fall was Romans, taught by Dr. Robert Jewett.

I was not particularly excited about studying Romans. All I knew about it was that it was abstract and heavily theological. I had become interested in the sociological and political contexts out of which the New Testament was written, and I didn't think Romans would be of much help in those areas.

Little did I know! The course began with a lecture on Phoebe and Paul's intended mission to Spain. I had forgotten that Paul even mentioned Spain in his letter and certainly had never even looked at a map to see why the Roman Christians were important to Paul's Spanish mission. Then we studied the names in Romans 16, and a whole new world opened up to me. I simply had no idea one could infer so much about the social situation of the earliest Christians.

When we begin in this way, we are less likely to fall into the trap of reading our own theology back into Romans. Nor are we dependent on Martin Luther to get at the key themes of Paul's letter. We can start with the Roman Christians themselves and try to figure out what Paul was saying to them. Only then can we translate his passionate message into meaning for our own lives today.

As I sat in class, I kept asking myself, "Why have I never heard this material in Sunday school?" I felt cheated. Did the curriculum writers never bother to find out about the latest research on Romans?

I realized later that research on the social world of the Bible is a fairly recent development, barely dreamed of when I was a student in high school and college. But a great deal of work has been done in the last thirty or forty years. Has that research become available to lay Christians in our churches? Unfortunately, not nearly enough.

Sitting in class, my question changed to "*Could* this material be taught in Sunday school?" and "*How* might it be done?" I have been trained as a teacher, and any new information that I find exciting, I want to share with others so they get turned on as well. If modern Christians could take on the roles of the earliest Christians in Rome, what might they learn from Paul that is otherwise missed? I began developing a curriculum in my head that eventually became my master's thesis. Using it, I taught Romans, or key parts of it, to various groups in the Chicago area.

After my idea was accepted for publication, Dr. Jewett asked me to take Romans with him again in 1992 and do further research and rewriting. Again I was amazed at the wealth of new material available on Romans and the social world of the New Testament in just the last four years. Some of my imaginative reconstructions had to be revised in light of these findings. The Jewish and Gentile Christians of Rome have become ever more alive to me as I follow them through the crowded streets of Rome and into their tiny apartments, as they work for kindly or harsh slavemasters or struggle to make a living as freed manual laborers or shopkeepers. I hear them argue with each other and watch them share Eucharist together with one risen Lord.

Understood this way, Romans becomes a marvelous blend of emphasis on spiritual depth and social justice, of union with Christ and unity among disparate people, of rightwising (see pages 73-74) through Jesus and holy living in community.

I acknowledge my debt to Dr. Robert Jewett, first for teaching Romans in such a way that it came alive to me, and then encouraging me while I wrote my own curriculum. When I received the offer for publication, he was even more ecstatic than I and suggested ways I might integrate the task of rewriting into my doctoral program.

I am also grateful to Dr. Linda Vogel, who teaches Christian Education at Garrett-Evangelical Seminary. After studying Romans, I took her course "Teaching the Bible" to learn more about writing curriculum. She was enormously supportive and enthusiastic and kept encouraging me to submit my work for publication. Both Drs. Jewett and Vogel are excellent teachers themselves. Some of their teaching methodology has become my own and is incorporated into this book.

I also owe much to the "guinea pig" students on whom I tried out my curriculum. The first group were the adults of Oak Park (Illinois) Mennonite Church, who participated in an 11-week course during Education Hour and helped me weed out some of the weaknesses. I realized more clearly what can and cannot be accomplished in a Sunday school setting. Another vital experience was teaching Romans to a seminary class at Eastern Mennonite Seminary in Harrisonburg, Virginia. Those students not only demonstrated the value of this material for those with some theological training, but also observed that this method of Bible study can be adapted even to two-thirds world situations where people are illiterate.

Additional thanks go to Dr. Virginia Wiles at New Brunswick Theological Seminary, who developed a website of Resources for Simulation of Roman House Churches for her students at http://www.nbts.edu/academics/faculty/wiles/romans/simul.htm and who graciously has invited all who read this book to make use of its resources.

First and last, I am indebted to my parents, Wilmer M. Halteman and Perle Guntz Halteman, to whom this book is dedicated. They introduced me to the treasures in the Bible, sometimes with unusual interpretations — and often with a great deal of humor!

RETA HALTEMAN FINGER

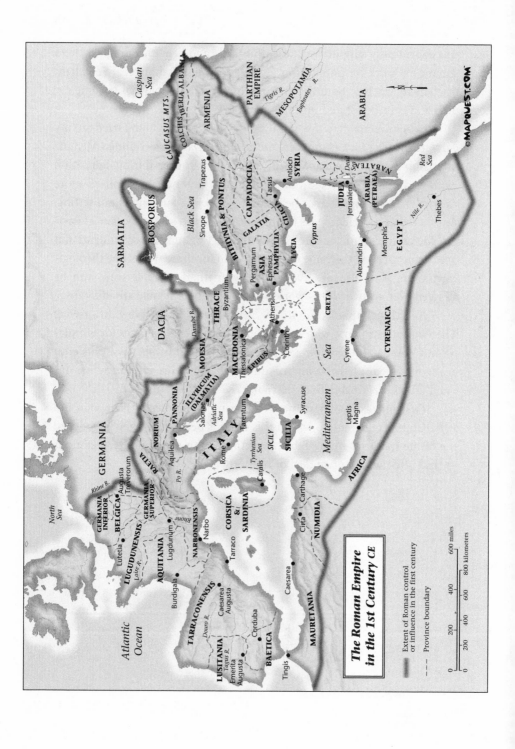

The Roman Empire
in the 1st Century CE

— Extent of Roman control
or influence in the first century

--- Province boundary

1 | A Special Visit to Rome

It was a Sabbath morning in April of A.D. 57. An air of excitement pervaded the large house on one of the Aventine hills in Rome. The house belonged to a Christian couple named Prisca and Aquila, and for the past few days they had been entertaining an unusual guest — Phoebe of Cenchreae. As the owner of a shipping business and a deacon of the church in Cenchreae, 800 miles to the southeast, Phoebe's long trip combined business with a spiritual mission. She had brought a letter for all the Christians in Rome from a well-known evangelist who called himself "Apostle to the Gentiles" — Paul of Tarsus.

Today Phoebe's secretary would read this letter to all the believers in the house church headed by Prisca and Aquila.

*　　*　　*

After a briefer-than-usual time of singing and reading Scripture, the believers ate a simple meal, celebrating the Eucharist as usual. For some, the presence of the risen Christ seemed even closer as they anticipated hearing Paul's words especially for them. Others felt wary. Would Paul disapprove of their conduct? Would he ask for favors from them? Why was he writing to Christians in Rome anyhow, since he had never been there?

But for every listener it was a festive occasion, an afternoon of entertainment in lives that knew mostly hard work from sunup to sundown. Would Paul's speech via Phoebe be as eloquent as the speech of a senator or of the Stoic philosophers in the marketplace? Prisca and Aquila had told them how powerfully Paul could preach when his emotions were stirred. All they could do was wait and see.

1

*   *   *

The day was finally over, and Phoebe was tired. For two hours her secretary had delivered Paul's speech to the Roman Christians. They had listened with rapt attention, and hours of discussion followed. A few had grasped Paul's argument immediately; most believers needed her further explanation and interpretation. Some were immediately enthusiastic, others needed more time for reflection, still others expressed reservations.

Nevertheless, the reception of Paul's letter was generally positive, as she knew it would be at this house church. Paul had lived with Prisca and Aquila in Corinth while they were exiled from Rome. Now back home again, they had taught believers under their care the theological truths that Paul had stressed.

But what about the other Christian cell groups in Rome? Paul had charged that she present the letter there, too. How would they receive it? Some, she knew, insisted that the Jewish Law must be kept, down to the last festival and dietary restriction. Others felt that the Law had been done away with entirely, and they didn't even want to observe the Sabbath. It will be interesting to see what happens, she thought, as week after week I meet with a different group. Can the power of God bring these argumentative people into unity? Will Roman Christians be the instruments to take the gospel of Jesus Christ to the ends of the Roman Empire? All she could do was wait and see.

*   *   *

Over 1,900 years have passed since Phoebe of Cenchreae's visit to Rome. Paul's letter is still read in Christian worship services today, still studied and debated in Bible classes. Many Christians memorize verses or entire passages from it.

But how many of these later believers remember Phoebe, a church leader and influential patron, who took Paul's message where he himself could not go? How many of us take the effort to visualize the recipients of the letter and imagine their response to it? Contemporary letters or speeches are always more understandable when we know something about the author, the recipients or listeners, and the purpose of the communication. The same is true for ancient writings.

The intent of this book is to reflect on Paul's letter to the Romans as if we really were these Christians at Rome. Then, as we more clearly understand what Paul meant in a first-century milieu, we are better able to translate his meaning into our context in the twenty-first century.

In my experience, Paul's letter to the Romans has usually been taught as if it were only a set of doctrines or a theological treatise. For most of us, this seems boring and outdated. It may even mean we have been misunderstanding Romans. Current research has focused so much on the social setting of the New Testament writings that a new world of meaning has opened up.

This book is the result of my conviction that lay Christians deserve to be let in on the secrets that biblical scholars are discovering and which make Bible study so much more informative and exciting.

A second important reason for studying Romans is to find out if Paul's message is helpful for us today. Paul wrote to the Roman Christians because they were racially and culturally diverse and he believed that the gospel of Christ had the power to break down those dividing walls between Jews and Gentiles, conservatives and liberals. Many churches today are hamstrung by disagreements between members who tend to be more "conservative" and others who may be more "liberal" (on whatever the current issue happens to be). Sometimes those on one side do not believe those on another side are even Christians. Energy goes into arguing or fighting, energy better used in outreach and mission. Instead, experiencing unity in our diversity could be a powerful witness to those observing the congregation from the outside.

Other church groups struggle with cultural diversity. Some are actively or passively racist. Paul's letter to the Romans speaks directly to these issues. As we learn about the house-church groups in Rome, we can better grasp Paul's understanding of the gospel and the grace and tolerance that flows from it. Then we can see how to apply that same gospel to our own congregational life.

The Structure of This Book

It is not only important to consider *what* we learn but *how* we learn. And sometimes the way we learn *least* is by sitting in a class and letting an "expert" stand up front and do all the talking. Even if the message reaches our heads, it often will not penetrate our hearts or our stomachs or our legs. It will never become an integral part of our lives.

Consequently, I have written this book not only to be read individually, but so that it can be used with groups of people.

A group can create a sustained simulation of one or more of the first-century Roman house churches who received Paul's letter. To do so, each person assumes the character of one member — Jew or Gentile; man or woman; slave, freedperson, or freeborn; rich or poor; conservative or liberal. Each character will also have an occupation and a particular role in his or her house church.

Then "Phoebe" comes and presents Paul's letter, a brief section at a time, since we do not have the patience of those who lived before the age of television! Each member of a house church stays in character and listens to what Paul says and decides how to react to it. Since Paul's letter would not have been considered Scripture at that time, it did not carry the same authority it was given later. No doubt many first-century Christians disagreed with Paul in major or minor ways. Thus our simulation allows for disagreement — which will make for lively discussion.

The simulation is followed by debriefing. The time machine turns off, and we are ourselves 1,900 years later. We can evaluate what happened in the simulation. Did we stay in character? How did the discussion help us understand what Paul meant? Do Paul's passionate convictions make sense for our lives today? If not, what has changed? What aspects of Paul's message *are still vital* for Christians of our century?

The following chapters are structured so the book can be used for a group as well as for individual study. Guidelines for simulation leaders are found in the "Leader's Guide" (appendix 1).

How Should We Interpret Romans?

There have been many ways to study Romans. Until recently, most scholars did not pay a great deal of attention to the historical setting of the letter. Romans is laid out rather systematically and theologically, so many have seen it primarily as Paul's most comprehensive explanation of the gospel, written near the end of his life. The identity of the recipients has not been considered very important.

All of us, whether we know it or not, have been greatly influenced by the way Martin Luther interpreted Romans — as a clear explanation of the great doctrine of justification by faith. Even more recently, Günther Bornkamm, a well-known Lutheran scholar who died in 1990 and whose life spanned most of the twentieth century, called Romans Paul's "last will and testament." In an essay he published in 1963, he wrote,

> This great document, which summarizes and develops the most important themes and thoughts of the Pauline message and theology and which elevates his theology above the moment of definite situations and conflicts into the sphere of the eternally and universally valid, this letter to the Romans is the last will and testament of the Apostle Paul.[1]

In our Christian education, most of us have learned about Romans as containing doctrines that were "eternally and universally valid." Some have memorized portions of Romans on how to be saved, texts that our teachers and ministers felt were among the clearest explanations to be found anywhere in the Bible. When my son was in junior high, he attended a youth group at a nearby evangelical church. His youth leader was planning to take the kids on a service mission with Native Americans in Oklahoma that summer, so he required all of them to learn the "Romans Road." This was a collection of verses, mostly from chapters 9 and 10,

1. Gunther Bornkamm, "The Letter to the Romans as Paul's Last Will and Testament," *Australian Biblical Review* 11 (1963): 2-14; see also his "The Letter to the Romans as Paul's Last Will and Testament," in *The Romans Debate*, ed. Karl P. Donfried (Peabody, Mass.: Hendrickson, 1991), 16-28.

which explain how to be saved. The youth leader wanted the kids to know these verses for any witnessing they might do in Oklahoma.

There is no doubt that Romans does talk about personal salvation, and that truths in it can be directly applied to our own lives today. However, when we ignore the historical situation in which a particular document was written, we can easily misinterpret all or parts of it, and many people can get hurt as a consequence. A good example is Romans 13:1-7, where Paul tells the Roman Christians to obey their rulers. This is sometimes used by people in power to oppress those they govern by saying that it is God's will that people should submit to their rulers. When we understand the situation among the Roman Christians in A.D. 57, we will interpret this text quite differently.

Fortunately, within the last thirty some years, much more historical research has been done on the life of Paul and on his letters to various churches, especially to the churches in Rome. There is a renewed interest in looking at parts of the biblical texts that most people ignored — introductions and conclusions, greetings to friends and co-workers, cultural details not immediately understood. Biblical scholars are now reconstructing the events of Paul's life as a missionary and learning more about ancient Jewish and Greco-Roman culture. In far more detail, they are sketching the situation of those Roman Christians and why Paul would have written to them.

Not all scholars agree, of course. One debate has centered around Romans 16, the concluding chapter, in which Paul introduces Phoebe and sends greetings to twenty-nine people. How, one might ask, could Paul know so many people in Rome when he had never been there himself? Since a few of the oldest manuscripts of Romans stop at the end of chapter 14, it was thought that chapter 16 was originally a part of a letter Paul wrote to the Ephesians. Paul had lived for quite some time in Ephesus, as had Prisca and Aquila, who are the first people he greets in chapter 16. Since he would have had many acquaintances there, some scholars felt it seemed logical to conclude that Romans 16 was really part of an Ephesian letter.

But no one can explain what happened to the rest of the Ephesian letter and *why* a conclusion of one letter would have been taken off and attached to another letter. In 1977, Harry Gamble, Jr., published *A Textual His-*

tory of the Letter to the Romans,[2] in which he carefully examines each existing manuscript of Romans and concludes that chapter 16 definitely belongs
to the Romans letter. Many scholars today have accepted this conclusion.

One well-known New Testament scholar, F. F. Bruce, did extensive
study on Romans during the 1970s and in 1981 gave a lecture on Paul's
purpose in writing to the Romans,[3] showing how much the letter was tied
to a specific historical situation. Since then other New Testament scholars
like Robert Jewett and Peter Lampe have added many more details which
greatly help us reconstruct the situation of the early Roman congregations.

The assumption that chapters 15 and 16 are part of Paul's original letter to the Romans is essential for our simulation, since it will be structured
around the groups and names to which Paul refers in Romans 16. This contrasts with more typical Bible studies that tend to skip over names of persons and places because they seem boring and irrelevant.

What kind of information can we learn from lists of names? Peter
Lampe has worked extensively on the names and groups of people greeted
by Paul in Romans 16. Following are a few examples of the things he has
observed.[4]

1. *Aristobulus and Narcissus were not Christians.* In Romans 16:10 and
11, Paul says, "Greet those who belong to the household of Aristobulus,"
and "Greet those in the household of Narcissus who are in the Lord"
(NIV). If either of these men had been Christians, Paul would have greeted
these heads of households themselves. Those Christians who were part of
those households, then, must be either slaves or former slaves working to
serve the interests of the owner of the (obviously large) estates.

2. *Women and men.* Verses 3 to 16 name twenty-six Christians in Rome

2. Harry Gamble, Jr., *A Textual History of the Letter to the Romans,* Studies and Documents, 42 (Grand Rapids: Eerdmans, 1977).

3. Printed in *The Romans Debate,* 175-194.

4. Peter Lampe, "The Roman Christians of Romans 16," in *The Romans Debate,* 216-
230. This article is dependent on his book *Die stadtrömischen Christen in den ersten beiden
Jahrhunderten: Untersuchen zur Sozialgeschichte* (Tübingen: J. C. B. Mohr, 1989). E. T. *From
Paul to Valentinus: Christians at Rome in the First Two Centuries,* trans. Michael Steinhauser
(Minneapolis: Fortress, 2003).

— nine women and seventeen men. But who, asks Lampe, is praised for being especially active in the church? More women than men! Seven women are given some title or compliment: being a co-worker with Paul (Prisca), working hard in the Lord (Mary, Tryphaena, Tryphosa, Persis), being as a mother to Paul (the mother of Rufus), or being of note among the apostles (Junia). Five men receive praise: being co-workers (Aquila, Urbanus), being approved in Christ (Apelles), being chosen in the Lord (Rufus), or being of note among the apostles (Andronicus). Already we can see that women have important roles of leadership in congregational life.

3. *The divided nature of Roman Christianity.* In chapter 16, Paul identifies five different groups, as well as naming some individuals who do not seem to belong to any of these groups. Clearly, the Roman Christians do not all worship together. In fact, Paul calls only one group an actual house church — the one headed by Prisca and Aquila (16:3-5). The others may have been cell groups, little pockets of Christianity scattered around Rome. Some of their theology and religious practices may have been quite different, as we shall see later.

Lampe has done much more research on first-century Rome and the Roman Christians. In our simulation we will be using his findings, which will give us more hints about critical problems there and why Paul wrote the sort of letter he did.

Models of Interpretation

The sociohistorical model which I am using to help us interpret Romans is obviously not the only one available today. Most of us are exposed primarily to what might be called the "doctrinal model." That perspective sees the Bible as containing timeless truths clearly set forth for people in any age and culture. When we study the New Testament following the doctrinal model, we tend to read it "on the flat," without taking much time to understand the actual historical and social situation out of which a text was written. This can lead to wrong interpretations, some of which have been and can be very hurtful. For those interested in other alternatives, see appendix 2, "Models of Biblical Interpretation."

2 | Why Did Paul Write to the Roman Christians?

Welcome to first-century Rome! Welcome to cool marble floors in upper-class homes, and to tiny rooms in tenements where families crowd together to sleep, talk, and eat. Welcome to the Via Appia, one of the main roads into the city, where transport animals bray and vehicles creak and rumble day and night. Welcome to the polluted waterfront of the Tiber River, where dockworkers and fisherwomen and fishermen eke out a living. Walk down the narrow, twisting streets to search in tiny shops and booths for necessities and luxury items. Step into small rooms where slave administrators and bookkeepers record transactions on papyrus for their imperial masters.

This is the Rome of A.D. 57, where small groups of believers met to pray and share table fellowship celebrating the risen Christ. Many of them were slaves or lower-class freedpersons; most could not read. A few were middle or upper class, some may have been upwardly mobile slaves working in imperial households. Some were Jews; most were Gentiles. Some tended to be "conservative" and moral; others tended to be "liberal" and loose-living. Those in one cell group may have had reasons for rivalry or hostility toward those in other cell groups.

By modern standards, this was a motley crew to whom Paul wrote. Yet he praises them as "full of goodness, filled with all knowledge, and able to instruct one another" (15:14). He sent them his most carefully structured theological letter — a letter that addressed real-life and more general situations, that was both a conversation and a treatise.[1] By simulating the his-

---

1. *The New Oxford Annotated Bible: New Revised Standard Version* (New York: Oxford University Press, 1991), 206 NT.

torical situation in which Paul's letter arrived, you can get a glimpse of Paul's original audience. Then you will be much better equipped to understand how Paul's passionate message applies to our lives today.

Why Did Paul Write Romans?

When Paul wrote to the Roman Christians, he had never been to Rome. Why did he write to them? Read Romans 15:15-29. As you read, ask yourself these questions:

1. *Why would Paul want to go to Rome if the gospel had already arrived there? Doesn't Paul say in 15:20-21 that he doesn't want to go where Christ has already been named?*

2. *How might the Roman churches be connected with Paul's desire to preach the gospel in Spain (15:23-24)?* (Check the map on page xiv.)

3. *Why might the Spanish mission be different from previous missionary journeys of Paul?*

Paul was an ambitious man, burning with energy and convinced that God had called him to take the gospel from one end of the Roman Empire to the other. He already had preached in the eastern part of the Empire and felt that his work there was finished. He had founded churches, and now other Christians could continue building them. He was moving west, and his sights were set on Spain.

The map quickly tells us that Rome was geographically the appropriate base from which Paul could set out for Spain. As far as we know, Rome by then was the farthest point west which the gospel of Christ had reached. Judging by the groups mentioned in Romans 16, there were many Christians there. As the capital of the Empire, Rome administered its Spanish provinces. If Paul was going to need help in preaching the gospel in Spain, it would have to come from Rome.

In what specific ways could the Roman Christians help Paul's mission to Spain? We may first think of financial aid, especially transportation costs. But most of the Roman Christians were either slaves or poor freedmen and freedwomen with no capital. Prisca and Aquila apparently have a home large enough for a church to meet there (Rom. 16:5) and may have been wealthier. But if Paul would have needed money from them, he could have written to them individually, without writing so carefully and comprehensively to all the Christians in Rome.

Robert Jewett thinks it is more likely that Phoebe, the church leader who brings the letter to Rome, is providing the funds for Paul's mission.[2] In Romans 16:2 he calls her a "patron" or "benefactor," a specific title for those of higher social status than the recipient or client. Such patrons used their influence to help or protect their clients in exchange for other services.[3] As a patron, Phoebe would have been wealthy and politically influential,[4] serving as Paul's benefactor in exchange for services he was providing for her, such as his proclamation and teaching of the gospel.

So, if it wasn't money Paul needed from the Christians in Rome for his missionary project, what was it? Likely he needed assistance with specific logistical problems arising from cultural, language, and political barriers.

We know from the book of Acts that when Paul entered a new city to preach the gospel, he first visited Jewish synagogues (Acts 13:5, 14; 14:1; 16:13; etc.) and apparently stayed in Jewish homes and practiced his trade as a tentmaker. It was the natural thing for him to do, since he was a Jew and was bringing the good news about the promised Jewish Messiah Jesus to his own people first. Some interested Gentiles hung around these syna-

---

2. Robert Jewett, "Paul, Phoebe, and the Spanish Mission," in *The Social World of Formative Christianity and Judaism*, ed. Jacob Neusner et al. (Philadelphia: Fortress, 1988), 142-161.

3. Richard P. Saller, *Personal Patronage Under the Early Empire* (Cambridge: Cambridge University Press, 1982), 7. Saller lists three vital elements involved in patronage: (1) the *reciprocal* exchange of goods and services; (2) a personal relationship of some duration, not a commercial transaction in the marketplace; and (3) an asymmetrical relationship in the sense that the two parties are of unequal status and offer different kinds of goods and services in the exchange.

4. The Greek word *prostatis* has traditionally been translated "helper" when referring to Phoebe — a term which commonly has connotations of inferiority or lower status to the person being helped. Scholars, evangelical as well as otherwise, now recognize that the term means "patron," and in the first-century Roman context meant a person of higher social rank who was a benefactor to one of lower rank. The main reason Phoebe was called a "helper" and a "servant" (rather than "deacon," as *diakonon* is translated elsewhere in reference to males) is simply because Phoebe was a woman. Male-oriented translators and theologians could not imagine a woman being in an equal or superior position to Paul, or being in a position of leadership at all.

gogues as well (Acts 13:43, "devout converts to Judaism"). When Jews would reject Paul's message, he would preach to these Gentiles, who often responded more favorably.

But a significant discovery was made recently by W. P. Bowers. There is no evidence that Jews lived in Spain until after the Jewish-Roman War of 66-70, after Paul's death.[5] Thus Paul's missionary strategy, his method of finding business contacts to financially support himself, and even the content of his message, would all have to be adapted in order to communicate with Roman and Spanish pagans.

Language was another barrier. Paul's native tongue was Greek, and Greek was the missionary language of the church. The Scriptures (our Old Testament) had not yet been translated into Latin, to say nothing of early Christian creeds, hymns, and stories. But Greek was not used in Spain. Only Latin was spoken in cities on the coasts and river valleys where Romans had colonized. Native Spanish dialects would still have been used inland.[6]

In the capital city of Rome, with its enormous diversity and many possibilities, Paul evidently believed he could find enough help to begin his mission to Spain. As we shall see later, two of the house-church groups were apparently part of imperial households. Some of the Christians may have been administrators for the emperor and thus able to provide Paul with connections or advise him on strategy. They would also have been proficient in Latin and able to translate essential material from Greek.

But there is another reason why Paul wrote to *all* the Roman Christians — poor and not-so-poor, Jew and Gentile, slave and free, men and women. As he understood the gospel, the core of its message was that *everyone*, no matter who they were, could come to God through Jesus Christ. The *very meaning of the gospel* lay in breaking down walls of hostility and division between people. In spite of great diversity, unity could be experienced in Christ.

However, the truth was that the Roman Christians were not com-

5. W. P. Bowers, "Jewish Communities in Spain in the Time of Paul the Apostle," *Journal of Theological Studies* 26 (1975): 395-402.

6. Jewett, "Paul, Phoebe, and the Spanish Mission," 145-147.

pletely unified. Romans 14 and 15 talk specifically about the "strong" and the "weak," and how they are quarreling about what to eat and what kind of holy days to observe. The very fact that they were divided into at least five different groups without a central location helps to explain why beliefs and practices were different and why rivalry existed.

Thus the problems Paul must have faced when planning for his Spanish mission were these:

1. *Theologically*, how can he preach a gospel that breaks down walls of hostility between people if those walls still exist among the Roman Christians?

2. *Practically*, how can he ask for unified support of his mission when people are so divided? If he receives the support of one group — say, more "liberal" Gentiles — does that mean more "conservative" Jews will try to undermine that support? Or vice versa? Before his mission even started, he'd be embroiled in messy religious politics. That, Paul would insist, is antithetical to the gospel itself.

The Roots of Conflict

Is there a particular reason why there might have been so many tensions between Jews and Gentiles in Rome? A look at the history of Jews living in Rome provides an important background for our study.

Ever since the Babylonians conquered Jerusalem in 597 and 586 B.C., large numbers of Judeans (Jews) had lived in other parts of the world besides Israel (2 Kings 24–25; Jer. 44). They were called Jews of the Diaspora, the dispersed. One might think that once they were so far away from their native land and their temple worship, they might have tended to forget their religious faith and melted in with the Gentiles. That certainly happened to some, but for many the opposite was true. Not having temple and land, they drew together in communities around the Law of Moses, the Torah. Keeping this Law — especially circumcision, dietary laws, and the Sabbath — became central to their lives and established their separate identity.

Some Jews of the Diaspora may have been even more conservative than those at the center of Judaism in Jerusalem, since they could not keep in as close touch with changes happening in the homeland. (This compares to the religious conservatism of people in the Appalachian hills, often quite cut off from the mainstream of their denominations, or to small Mennonite or Hutterite communities in rural areas.)

The Jewish Diaspora in the East, where Paul had been evangelizing, had existed for centuries. Though the Jewish community in Rome was comparatively young when Paul wrote his letter, it had a history of decentralization and uneasy relationships with the government. From Wolfgang Wiefel's essay on the Jewish Community in ancient Rome,[7] I have highlighted major events which bear on our study of Paul's letter.

The presence of Jews in Rome was not mentioned until 139 B.C. Later they were expelled because the ruling upper-class Romans, suspicious of all things foreign, mistook the Jews for a hellenistic-oriental cult.

Between 50 and 40 B.C., many Jews were brought to Rome as captives of war. Soon after, a large group of them were freed, and they settled on the left bank of the Tiber River. Anti-Semitism developed as the Romans — especially Cicero, a leading senator — became appalled at the "barbaric, superstitious" religion of the Jews and would sometimes see it as a threat to Roman traditions. Because of their annual payment of taxes to the temple in Jerusalem, the Jews were accused of transferring funds abroad. From then on, there were numerous political shifts between toleration and opposition.

In A.D. 19, anti-Semitism sprang up again, and the emperor Tiberius expelled thousands of Jews from Rome. The Jewish community was hit hard but not destroyed. As time passed, many synagogues sprang up. Recent study of Jewish inscriptions on buildings and tombs has shown that the inner structure of each worshiping congregation (synagogue) was similar, but that there was no centralization of authority. This had repercussions for the future of Christianity in Rome.

The church was born at Pentecost and spread out from Jerusalem during the mid-30s A.D. Rome became the first city in the western Mediter-

---

7. Wolfgang Wiefel, "The Jewish Community in Ancient Rome and the Origins of Roman Christianity," in *The Romans Debate*, 85-101. Also see W. Sanday and A. C. Headlam, *The Epistle to the Romans,* International Critical Commentary (New York: Charles Scribner's Sons, 1915), xviii-xxv.

ranean where Christianity took hold. This was possible because of the loose structure of Judaism there. The many congregations, their democratic constitutions, and the absence of a central Jewish governing board made it easy for Christian missionaries to preach in synagogues and win converts. These converts worshiped with traditional Jews, and frictions developed.

During the late 40s, the Jews apparently rioted because of their different beliefs about Christ. This came to the attention of the emperor Claudius. Influenced by the riots and by the past history of anti-Semitism, and not able to turn to a central Jewish authority to mediate the dispute, Claudius in 49 expelled all Jewish leaders, both Christians and traditional Jews, and forbade clubs and meetings in synagogues (Acts 18:2).[8] Of those Christians who remained, a majority would have been Gentiles or lower-class, low-profile Jews. Since they could no longer meet with Jews in the synagogues, they began meeting in private homes or tenement apartments.

In 54, Nero came to power. More pro-Jewish than Claudius, Nero allowed the edict of expulsion to lapse, and Jews began returning to Rome in great numbers. Jewish Christians came back to find Christian house congregations with Gentile leadership — a completely different organizational structure and likely some change in spiritual outlook. Apparently some Gentiles were not accepting the Jews back into their congregations. During their absence, the Jewish Christians also changed, for many could have been influenced by Paul's emphasis on freedom from the Law.[9] The stage was set for friction and struggle.

Two or three years later, in 56 or 57, Paul wrote to all the Roman Christians to urge toleration and unity.

There are two important points to remember from this brief sketch: (1) the long history of friction between Jews and Roman Gentiles, and (2) the major recent event of the expulsion of Jews and their gradual return to Rome. All this would certainly have contributed to the difficulty of Christian Jews and Gentiles getting along together in unity. This background will be an important factor as you simulate the church groupings in Rome and listen to Paul's letter.

8. Sanday and Headlam, *The Epistle to the Romans*, xxi.
9. Wiefel, "Jewish Community in Ancient Rome," 94.

3 | Establishing House Churches in Rome

Who were these Roman Christians, and what were their house churches like? Turn to Romans 16:3-16. Among the many names Paul mentions, those most prominent are of individuals whom Paul seems to know personally. He identifies them by a word of praise, such as "Greet Mary, who has worked very hard among you," and "Greet Urbanus, our co-worker in Christ." There are sixteen of these friends. Since Paul knows them personally, or at least knows something about them, most likely they are some of the Jewish refugees expelled from Rome in A.D. 49, and now returning.

These returnees, with the exception of Prisca and Aquila, are not clearly attached to any house church or cell group. However, Epaenetus (E-pa-NEET-us) (16:5b) may be part of the house church of Prisca and Aquila. Perhaps he was converted by them, joined their business, and returned with them from Asia.[1] And Herodion (he-ROAD-i-on) (16:11) may be connected with the household of Aristobulus (a-ris-TO-bu-lus). But mostly these returning refugees have not yet adjusted to the different congregational situation in Rome, nor perhaps have the present cell groups made much effort to accept them back.

Now Paul greets *five groups* of people:

- In 16:5a we hear about the church meeting in the house of Prisca and Aquila.
- In 16:10b, Paul greets "those who belong to the household of Aristobulus" (NIV).[2]

1. James D. G. Dunn, *Romans 9–16*, Word Biblical Commentary, vol. 38B (Waco, Tex.: Word Books, 1988), 893.
2. Although the NRSV uses the term "family" instead of "household" (NIV), the lat-

- In 16:11b, he addresses "those in the household of Narcissus who are in the Lord" (NIV).
- In 16:14, five persons without description are greeted by name, including other "brothers and sisters who are with them."
- In 16:15, five others are named or referred to, along with "all the saints who are with them."

These five groups appear to be congregations of Christians scattered throughout Rome of whom Paul is aware through his contacts. He does not know them personally, since he had not yet visited Rome. But Paul does know Prisca and Aquila since they were two of the many victims of Claudius' edict of expulsion (Acts 18:2). In both Corinth and Ephesus, Paul had worked with them before they returned to Rome.

These five groups, along with the returning Jewish Christian refugees, received Paul's letter in 56 or 57. As readers of this book and participants in the simulation, you will be learning about Paul's message through the ears and eyes of characters in these early Christian cell groups in Rome.

Social and Theological Profiles of the Five House Churches

The first chapter included a few examples from Peter Lampe's work of what we can learn from the names in Romans 16. From Lampe's research and others such as Heikki Solin, who compiled and analyzed thousands of Greek names from Roman archaeology and history, Robert Jewett has prepared a social and theological profile of each of these house churches.[3] Much of the following information is derived from his reconstructions. We should keep in mind that, though we cannot be 100 percent certain about these profiles, neither are they simply created out of imagination.

---

ter is more accurate, since households in the Roman Empire included the extended family plus clients, servants, and slaves.

3. These profiles are drawn from Robert Jewett's *Romans*, Cokesbury Basic Bible Commentary (Nashville: Graded Press, 1988), 147-148; and Jewett's unpublished lecture, "'To All God's Beloved in Rome': A Cross-Cultural Analysis of the Recipients of Paul's Letter," March 24, 1988.

When different types of data are put together, patterns develop and probabilities can be suggested. In order to set up a rounded-out simulation, we have to operate on both facts and probabilities.

The Church in the House of Prisca and Aquila (16:3-5)

This house church is the only one of the five mentioned in Romans 16 that is actually called a church. Perhaps Prisca and Aquila, as patrons, are the only ones wealthy enough to have a home large enough to handle a congregation. The other groups may be more aptly called "cell groups" who met in tiny tenement apartments.

Excavations on the Prisca catacomb in Rome link Prisca's name with an upper-class, noble family called Acilius (a-SIL-i-us). In A.D. 91, a member of this family, M. Acilius Glabrio, was executed for atheism in Rome. Apparently his Christian sympathies were discovered, since atheism was a common charge against those who worshiped Jesus as Lord instead of Caesar.

In addition, Prisca's name was discovered underneath the Santa Prisca Church, which had apparently been built on the site of her home. This was in the Aventine (A-ven-tine), in an area of Rome where many elegant first-century homes were located. If these excavations have been interpreted correctly, it would explain how Prisca and Aquila, after returning to Rome so recently, could own a house large enough for a worshiping congregation. Prisca's noble status in society, along with her apparent teaching skills, may also account for her name usually being mentioned before Aquila's in the New Testament.

Aquila's name is the Greek form of Acilius, which meant that he was somehow connected to the Roman Acilius family. Acts 18:2-3 tells us that Aquila was a Jewish tentmaker, which in the Roman context probably meant awning maker.[4] Wealthy, upper-class people considered labor of any kind, including the skilled trades, socially beneath them, so Aquila may have originally been a slave or client of the Acilius family. Their marriage must have been quite atypical — a true love-match — since nobility did not usually

4. Lampe, *Die stadtrömischen Christen,* 157-158.

marry those of the lower classes. Although Aquila maintained his tent-making business, the income would not have supported their lifestyle in a large house, so Prisca must have had money and significant social status.

There is a biblical clue that both Prisca and Aquila were full Roman citizens — a special privilege in those days. Paul says in Romans 16:4 that they "risked their necks" for his life. First, this implies that they had the po-litical clout to intercede for him with hostile governmental authorities during one of his arrests and imprisonments. Paul was thus indebted to them, his patrons. Second, only Roman citizens had the right to a death penalty by beheading. Noncitizens could be tortured, crucified, or thrown to wild animals in the arena.

We know about Prisca (Priscilla) and Aquila's previous work with Paul from Acts 18:1-4, 18-21, and 24-28. Thus the church in their house was probably an egalitarian congregation with a Pauline theology and a racial mixture of Jews, Greeks, and Romans. Yet their household in this first-century Roman context would have been composed of members of the larger Acilius family, along with clients, freedpersons, and slaves under their patronage.

Extra names for simulation: *Greek male* — Soullios (SUL-i-us), Nektarios (nek-TAR-i-os). *Greek female* — Dorea, Aurelia (au-REEL-i-a), Theotekna (thee-o-TEK-na). *Latin male* — Cuspius, Olympius, Sextus. *Latin female* — Clariana, Felicia, Rustica.

Those of the Household of Aristobulus (16:10)

It is clear from the above expression that Aristobulus himself is not a Christian, but some members of his household are. Who is Aristobulus? The name is non-Roman, so he is likely an immigrant. Several commenta-tors have suggested that Aristobulus is the grandson of Herod the Great (who massacred the babies when Jesus was born) and brother of Agrippa I (who ruled during Paul's lifetime; Acts 12).[5] He had lived in Rome, was a

---

5. J. B. Lightfoot, *St. Paul's Epistle to the Philippians* (London and Cambridge: Macmillan, 1873), 172-173; Sanday and Headlam, *The Epistle to the Romans*, 425; Dunn, *Romans 9–16*, 896.

friend of the emperor Claudius, and died in 44. Even though he was dead by the time Paul wrote his letter, his household had likely been united with the imperial household, and his slaves would have continued to be called by the name of their former owner.[6]

Comments Jewett, "The profile of this Christian cell would thus feature upwardly mobile Greek and Jewish administrators whose careers depended on loyalty to the emperor. Even as low-level bureaucrats in the Claudian and Neronian administrations, they would have prospects of career advancement [and] financial security. The orientation of this particular group would likely be pro-Roman, pro-Jewish, and anti-zealotic, consistent with the Herodian outlook."[7]

Significantly, the person Paul greets next as his relative (therefore a Jew) is Herodion, which lends support to the above thesis. His name suggests that he is either a slave or a freedman of the Herod family. It is not clear whether Herodion is already a member of the *Aristobuliani* (a-rist-o-bul-ē-AN-ē) or whether Paul is suggesting that they accept him into their cell group. He may have been a Jewish freedman who was expelled under Claudius and is now returning to his former household.

Possible names for members: *Male* — Eutuchas (U-tu-kas), Demetrius (de-ME-tri-us), Herodes (her-O-des), Isidoros (i-si-DOOR-os). *Female* — Kalandia (kal-AND-i-a), Gaia (GĪ-a), Pollitta (pol-E-ta), Suria (Soo-ri-a).

Those of the Household of Narcissus (16:11)

Like Aristobulus, it is unlikely that Narcissus was a Christian. Narcissus was a name common among slaves and freedmen.[8] However, if this was a famous person like Aristobulus, the most likely candidate is the powerful freedman who was Claudius's chief secretary and whose wealth was proverbial, according to the Roman satirist Juvenal.[9] Narcissus's fortunes had

6. Lightfoot, *St. Paul's Epistle to the Philippians*, 173.
7. Jewett, "'To All of God's Beloved,'" 10.
8. Dunn, *Romans 9–16*, 896.
9. Juvenal, *Satire* 14.329.

changed after Nero became emperor in 54, when Nero's mother Agrippina had forced Narcissus to commit suicide.[10] As was usual in those cases, his household then passed into the hands of the emperor but still retained the name of Narcissus.[11]

Thus those Christian *Narcissiani* (nar-sis-ē-AN-ē) would have approximately the same status as the *Aristobuliani* — slaves and freedmen who were highly trained, well-paid, upwardly mobile imperial bureaucrats. But Jewett sees the political and religious orientation of those of Narcissus as quite different from those of Aristobulus — "Greek slaves with Roman imperial loyalties, probably with a far less friendly attitude toward Judaism."[12]

Possible names for members: *Female* — Aelia (Ā-li-a), Caia (Kī-a), Diana, Gesatia (ge-SAT-i-a). *Male* — Aelius (Ā-li-us), Zoninus (zo-NĒ-nus), Caulius (KAW-li-us), Euporus (U-por-us), Gaudentius (gaw-DEN-ti-us).

The Brothers (16:14)

Paul calls this group "the brothers" (NIV), although the Greek word Paul uses, *adelphous,* usually means "brothers and sisters" (NRSV). All of the five men mentioned have names of Greek origin. This points to their status as slaves or freedmen, since persons with Greek names in first-century Rome were usually of servile origin.

Asyncritus, (a-SIN-cri-tus), found only once in Roman records of the second half of the first century, is based on a verbal adjective in Greek which means "incomparable." *Phlegon* (FLEH-gon) appears seven times in first-century Roman records; three references are for persons clearly of slave background. The name is Greek and was used earlier as a dog's name.[13] *Hermes* (HER-meez) was found 640 times in first-century Rome, usually as the name of a slave or freedman.

10. Roman historian Tacitus, *Annals* 13.1.

11. Lightfoot, *St. Paul's Epistle to the Philippians,* 173.

12. Jewett, "'To All of God's Beloved,'" 11.

13. C. E. B. Cranfield, *The Epistle to the Romans* (Edinburgh: T. & T. Clark, 1979), 795.

The Greek *Patrobas* (pa-TRŌ-bus) is not found at all in Roman records, but the Romanized "Patrobius" (pa-TRŌ-bi-us) occurs eight times,
four of them in the New Testament period. The Roman ending may indicate a desire not to be associated with slave status, since several men
named Patrobius were quite prominent freedmen.[14] However, the Greek
Patrobas of Romans 16:14 points to a man of lower social status. *Hermas*
(HER-mas) is also likely a slave name, since it is Greek and derived from
the god Hermes.

These men were probably the leaders of a cell group that seems to be
of low social status, since all five names are of slave origin. (Few slaves had
the privileges and opportunities of those who worked in imperial households, such as those of Narcissus and Aristobolus.) Regarding their orientation, notes Robert Jewett, "the selection of the title 'brothers' for this
group probably indicates an egalitarian ethos. However, the lack of feminine leaders seems to indicate a limit to the scope of equality."[15]

Names for women members: Dorea, Suria, Jucunda, Plotia.

The Saints (16:15)

The fifth Christian cell group is called "the saints," a term which may imply
a connection to conservative Jewish Christianity such as that in Jerusalem
(see 15:25-26). The names, however, are Greek. There are eighteen references
to *Philologus* (fil-OL-o-gus) in Roman materials from the New Testament
period, half of which are clearly to slaves or freedmen. *Julia* is the most frequently used of all the names in Romans 16. It was used over 1,400 times in
Roman records, mostly for women of servile origin, and frequently for
slaves and other women of the Julian households. (Julian households were
those of the emperors — Augustus, Tiberius, Caligula, Claudius, and Nero
— and others descended from Julius Caesar.) Commentators usually associate Philologus and Julia as husband and wife or brother and sister.[16]

---

14. Lampe, *Die stadtrömischen Christen,* 148.
15. Jewett, "'To All of God's Beloved,'" 12.
16. For example, Cranfield, *The Epistle to the Romans,* 795; Dunn, *Romans 9–16,* 898.

Nereus (NEER-e-us) is another common name coined for slaves, taken from Neptune, the Roman sea god. There are twenty-eight references to Nereus during the New Testament period. Statistically, this Nereus was likely a slave or freedman. *Nereus's sister* would have shared his social status. Paul evidently does not know her name, but he mentions her as one of the leaders among the Saints. *Olympas* (o-LIM-pas), a male name, is found only twice in Roman records, neither from the New Testament period. This name also points to slave background.

Was this cell group also part of an imperial household, as was the Aristobuliani and Narcissiani? It is possible but not as probable, given the frequency of names like Philologus and Julia. Because all these names are slave, this group could, like the Brothers, be of low social standing and reside in tenements in one of the slums of Rome. Jewett evaluates the religious outlook of this group as conservative "and possibly having a strong tie to Judaism; yet the prominence of feminine leadership points toward an egalitarian orientation."[17]

Extra names: *Female:* Tapontus (ta-PON-tus), Quarta, Hermione (her-MĪ-own-ee). *Male:* Lucius (LU-shus), Granius (GRAN-i-us), Vitalis (vi-TAL-is).

Re-creating the Roman House Churches

If you are part of a class studying Romans, at this point you will begin to re-create one or more of these house churches. Instructions for how to do this are included in the Leader's Guide in appendix 1. Persons should focus most on the sketch of their own group but should also know something about the other groups.

If you are reading this book by yourself, you may want to choose one group and develop a character or two from that group. If you sketch out two characters, one a Jew (conservative or liberal, man or woman, slave or free) and the other a Gentile with opposite characteristics, you can imagine how each would have reacted to Paul's letter.

17. Jewett, "'To All of God's Beloved,'" 14.

Below is an outline for a character sketch. Fill in this page with the name you have chosen, your house church, and your ethnic background — Jewish, Greek, or Latin. After reading the rest of this chapter and the next two, you can make more decisions about your character and fill in more of the sketch. Make your character as complex and interesting as possible!

Character Sketch

Name:

House church:

Ethnic background:

Ethnic and political sympathies (liberal, conservative, or whatever):

Location of house church in Rome:

Description of living quarters:

Occupation and specific role in occupation:

Previous religion and how you converted:

Role in cell group — spiritual gifts and responsibilities:

Moral strengths and weaknesses: pet peeves about other members of
   your house church or other groups:

Other personality characteristics:

A more detailed list of questions is in appendix 3 under "Creating Individual Characters for Role Play: Questions to Ask Yourself" on pp. 184-185. Sample character sketches and many other resources on ancient Rome can be found at a website created especially for this book by Virginia Wiles, a New Testament professor who has used this book to teach college or seminary classes. See www.nbts.edu/academics/faculty/wiles/romans/simul.htm

Housing for House Churches

What pictures come to mind as you envision a church congregation meeting in a large room in someone's home? Few of our homes today have living rooms that could contain more than twenty or thirty people. How did the Roman Christians manage it? Knowing something about the housing situation in first-century Rome makes the existence of house churches even more of a miracle.

The homes of the wealthy did have meeting space. In addition to private rooms and offices for the owner, women's and children's quarters, and slaves' quarters, the most important room was the dining room. Here the head of the household could entertain his peers, clients, and friends from other households.[18] A dining room in a typical villa measured approximately 400 square feet. This allowed room for nine people to recline on couches around the wall. If the couches were removed, perhaps twenty persons could gather. If the crowd overflowed into the adjoining atrium (central patio), and if all decorative urns were removed and some folks did not mind getting shoved into the shallow pool, fifty people might jam in. The maximum comfortable range was thirty to forty.[19]

However, most people did not enjoy such spacious homes. About 3 percent of the population of Rome occupied one-third of the residential space of the city. Most people were crowded into huge tenements called

18. Vincent Branick, *The House Church in the Writings of Paul* (Wilmington, Del.: Michael Glazier, 1989), 38-39.

19. These representative dimensions are taken from a villa near Corinth, part of the data collected by Jerome Murphy-O'Connor, *St. Paul's Corinth: Texts and Archaeology* (Wilmington, Del.: Michael Glazier, 1989), 155.

insulae.[20] The descriptions of the *regiones,* the fourteen administrative regions into which the emperor Augustus divided Rome, list only one private house for every twenty-six blocks of *insulae.*[21]

These tenements were four or five stories high, with dark rooms off long interior hallways. The higher one climbed, the smaller the rooms (even down to 30 or 35 square feet) and the cheaper the rent (no elevators!). Often the larger rooms of about 300 square feet on lower floors were subdivided so several families could share the rent. The *insulae* contained no central heating, no running water, and no toilet facilities.[22] They were often so poorly built that walls were in constant danger of collapsing. Some renters cooked over charcoal braziers in their rooms, and fire was an ever-present hazard. Other occupants were fed from a common kitchen.

In spite of these conditions, rents were high, especially in Rome. An average room rented for about 40 denarii a month. Since a common laborer's wage was generally one denarius a day, poorer families had to share space. By contrast, the largest rooms on the first floor of a tenement would rent for 625 denarii a month. Thus the average population density in the cities of the Empire equaled the density of the industrial slums in modern Western cities, about 200 persons per acre.[23]

To compensate for such misery, most cities devoted about one-fourth of their space to public facilities such as gardens, baths, and city squares. Most of the population, therefore, lived out of doors on streets and sidewalks with little privacy.[24] Housing was for sleeping and storing one's few belongings.

20. Branick, *The House Church,* 39.

21. Jerome Carcopino, *Daily Life in Ancient Rome: The People and the City at the Height of the Empire,* trans. from the French by E. O. Lorimer (New Haven: Yale University Press, 1940), 23.

22. Bruce W. Frier, *Landlords and Tenants in Imperial Rome* (Princeton: Princeton University Press, 1980), 15, 28.

23. Branick, *The House Church,* 42-43.

24. Branick, *The House Church,* 43.

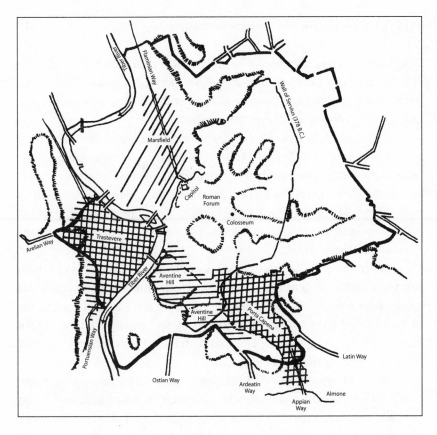

Christian House Churches in Rome

Locations for House and Tenement Churches

The accompanying sketch of Christian house churches in first-century Rome is based on a map developed by Peter Lampe.[25] He used literary evidence plus five different types of archaeological evidence to locate the precise districts where Christianity got its start.

The most likely areas for our Christian cell groups to have existed are in Trastevere (tras-TEV-er-e) and the section along the Appian Way around the Porta Capena, where many immigrants lived. Both Trastevere and Porta Capena were swampy areas where the poorest population of Rome lived. Trastevere was by the harbor. There lived harbor workers, warehouse laborers, seamen, brick and tile workers, potters, millers, tanners, and leatherworkers.

Trastevere was the most densely populated section of the city, with the most high-rise tenements and the fewest number of bakeries per square kilometer. It was full of immigrants from the East and was the site of shrines and temples for mystery cults. A few years later when Rome burned, Trastevere, across the Tiber River, did not. Perhaps because of this, Nero scapegoated the Christians.

The area around the Porta Capena was a damp valley with heavy traffic into the city. It was populated by traders, handworkers, and transport workers, such as donkey drivers and carriers — all of low social status. Transport work in Rome was at night, so sleeping was difficult day or night.

Two other districts indicate some Christian population, Marsfield and the Aventine Hill. Both may represent higher social status. The old Santa Prisca Church is in the Aventine. The area underneath it has been excavated, revealing large upper-class homes that date from the first century. Churches built after Constantine were often built on the site of homes owned by Christian patrons where house churches had met. In the Aventine, aristocrats lived on the hills where the air was cleaner. The poorer one was, the farther down the valley one lived.

Where would the first-century Christian groups in Rome have lived

25. Adapted from Lampe, *Die stadtrömischen Christen*, illustration 3.

and worshiped together? Based on what you have learned so far, can you make some deductions?

We have already learned that the most likely location for the home of Prisca and Aquila is in the Aventine, where they hosted a church in their house. Aside from other evidence, this fact alone assures their status as upper class and wealthy. However, many members of their church could have lived in small rooms on the top floors of their house, or in nearby tenements.

What about those from the households of Aristobulus and Narcissus? Since they worked in imperial households, it makes sense to also place them in the Aventine or in Marsfield. However, these believers were likely slaves who also lived in small rooms on upper floors of these wealthy homes.

Trastevere even today is the Jewish quarter of Rome and seems to have been for many centuries. In *The Agony and the Ecstasy,* Irving Stone notes that when Michelangelo was sculpting his famous Pieta in the early 1400s, he went to Trastevere to look for a Jewish woman to model Mary. So it makes sense to place the poor, more Jewish church of "The Saints" in Trastevere. "The Brothers," all or mostly Gentile, are likely to be found in the slums of Porta Capena.

*   *   *

If you are part of a group study, choose where your house church meets and write the information on your character sketch. Each group can then choose a name for their house church and design an appropriate sign to advertise it (see the Leader's Guide for more suggestions). Someone from each house church can then introduce it — and each member in it by name and racial origin — to the other groups.

Following are a few examples from first-year college classes:

- House church of Prisca and Aquila (awning-makers): "The dAwning of Christ"; "The House of Aventine: Where Caesar Is Just a Salad"
- Brothers and Sisters (cobblers): "Sole Siblings"; "Phlegon's Pheet Phleet"
- Saints (weavers and dyers): "Tye-Dyers of Trastevere"; "Dyeing Saints"

4 | Standing on the Bottom Rung: Hierarchy in Roman Society

We cannot re-create Roman house churches and understand many things about Paul's letter without some grasp of the social institutions that structured Roman society as a whole. Most North Americans are used to living in a democratic society where the large majority are middle class and have a fair measure of political and social freedom. Our continent is rich in natural resources and has not yet been overwhelmed by huge populations. Thus, our heritage has, at least until recently, implied that if we worked hard, we could get ahead, make money, and climb from one social class to the next.

Since 1863 slavery has been declared illegal in the United States, so theoretically every citizen has the right to "life, liberty, and the pursuit of happiness." These ideals of democracy come from our history books in school and shape our ideas of what culture is or should be like. Yet there are also crushing realities of poverty for many minority groups or deprived classes in North America, frightening economic forecasts for middle classes, and virtual slavery that millions around the world still experience.

However, even the ideal of universal democracy would have been unthinkable in first-century Rome. Only a tiny minority were upper class. The top *senatorial* class comprised about two-thousandths of one percent. The next order, *equestrians* (knights), probably amounted to less than a tenth of one percent.[1] Under them was a small *middle* class of other aristocracy, followed by the vast majority: *slaves* and relatively poor *freedpersons*.

---

1. Ramsay MacMullen, *Roman Social Relations: 50 B.C. to A.D. 284* (New Haven: Yale University Press, 1974), 88-89.

The aristocrats did not engage in commerce and industry, as do our middle classes. That was beneath their dignity. Ordinary labor was performed by those who had no choice but to make a living (or look for handouts) — free workers, freedpersons, and slaves. No Roman imagined a society without slaves, since they were the economic backbone of the Empire. Late in the first century, the slaves of Italy were estimated at two million out of a six-million population. For the whole Empire, 500,000 new slaves were needed each year from 50 B.C. to A.D. 150,[2] partly because some ran away and others were freed. Freedmen and freedwomen, though with more civil rights, could be worse off economically than when they had been enslaved.

Slavery was not based on race, as in our American past. There were at least four ways persons became slaves:

- Captured as victims of war.
- Through breeding. The child of a slave mother was also legally a slave. Children were often taken from slave mothers and raised by others, thus weakening family ties.[3]
- Through debt, when persons sold themselves or their children into slavery in order to survive.
- By exposure. Unwanted infants, especially girls, were thrown out but sometimes rescued by others and raised to be slaves.[4] Richer people thus limited family size to keep their wealth intact. Further, men married about ten years later than women, in their late twenties or early thirties.[5] Since the Romans placed little value on sexual abstinence, young unmarried men sexually exploited prostitutes or their own slaves. Many unwanted children resulted.

In spite of the prevalence of slavery, it was not always a permanent condition. There was a strong feeling that a loyal domestic servant ought to be granted freedom and some civil rights after a number of years. How-

2. K. R. Bradley, "On the Roman Slave Supply and Slavebreeding," in *Classical Slavery*, ed. M. I. Finley (London: Frank Cass & Co., 1987), 42-64.

3. Bradley, "On the Roman Slave Supply," 55.

4. Richard Saller, "Slavery and the Roman Family," in *Classical Slavery*, 69-70.

5. Saller, "Slavery," 68.

ever, an ex-slave was still expected to continue in a dependent relationship to his or her master, with the same deference children owed their parents. Such a slave still had economic obligations to the former master.[6] Unlike the American experience with slavery, there was a wide range of status and conditions among slaves. The majority worked on agricultural estates, a lesser number in mines, performing endless labor with no hope of freedom or of family life (marriage unions among slaves were not recognized).[7] Conditions in the mines were so deplorable that few slaves there survived more than a few years.

On the other hand, a comparatively few bright, ambitious slaves worked directly for the emperor and were highly trained in skills for administering the Empire.[8] They were valued because they had ties of loyalty to no one else and owed their entire career to the emperor. They were even allowed to marry citizen women. Slaves and freedpersons of this type were likely involved in Christian cell groups in the households of Aristobulus and Narcissus.

Let us now try to understand how our house-church groups with their mix of slaves, freed, and freepersons fit into the social structures of first-century Rome. Then you can further develop your own characters.

There were three major institutions of society:

- The city community, *politeia* (pol-i-TAY-a), from which comes our word *politics.*
- The household community, *oikonomia* (oi-kon-o-ME-a), from which we get our word *economics.*
- The voluntary association, *koinōnia* (koi-no-NEE-a), now an English loanword used for Christian fellowship, community, and small-group sharing.

---

6. Thomas Wiedemann, *Greek and Roman Slavery* (Baltimore: Johns Hopkins University Press, 1981), 3-4.

7. Wiedemann, *Greek and Roman Slavery*, 1, 8.

8. This was especially true for the Julio-Claudian emperors. Wiedemann, *Greek and Roman Slavery*, 9.

The *Politeia*

Because Christians met in homes rather than public buildings, the *politeia* did not as directly influence their day-to-day Christian living as the other two social institutions. The Roman Republic had been torn apart and the beginnings of a monarchy and centralized government established under Augustus (27 B.C.-A.D. 14). The common people had never experienced nor ever expected a government with democratic representation. Yet only when there were public disturbances, such as those which prompted Claudius's edict of expulsion for the Jews, did their religious beliefs become an issue in the *politeia*.

The book of Acts speaks of local uprisings or riots against Paul and his companions (as in Acts 16:16-24; 19:23-41). Later, when Nero was looking for scapegoats on which to blame Rome's great fire of 64, Roman Christians endured unspeakable suffering. But in the late 50s during the early years of Nero's reign when he was 19 or 20, older and wiser advisers governed the Empire and a relative calm prevailed.[9] We'll find out more about that later when we look at Romans 13:1-7.

The *Oikonomia*

The household was the primary structure of the Roman Empire. It was composed of a number of families or individuals bound together under the authority of the senior male of the principal family.[10] They would live on the same estate or in nearby tenements and be engaged in the same enterprise, such as agriculture, manufacturing, or trade. Generally women would work indoors, men outdoors.

---

9. M. Cary and H. H. Scullard, *A History of Rome Down to the Reign of Constantine* (London: Macmillan, 1975), 358. "During the ministry of Seneca and Burrus the government of Nero followed a cautious but efficient administrative routine. The emperor's pranks as yet did not give rise to serious scandal, and outside his own family he had spilt hardly any blood. But the death of Burrus in 62, followed by the retirement of Seneca, . . . marked a turning-point in Nero's reign."

10. Derek Tidball, *The Social Context of the New Testament: A Sociological Analysis* (Grand Rapids: Zondervan, 1984), 79-80.

There was a clear hierarchy of authority, culminating in the absolute power of the male head of the family. The father even had life or death power over any children born to him. If he did not pick up his infant son or daughter when it was presented to him at birth, it was taken out and exposed on one of the city's garbage dumps.

All sons accepted into the family were under the authority of their father until he died, no matter how old. Depending on what form of marriage was involved, daughters either remained under their father's authority all their lives or at marriage were passed on to their husband's authority.[11] The oldest son, as the male heir, assumed a place of paramount importance in the family and household. If there was no son, the father had the power to adopt a son and make him his heir. Such adoption was common and was a treasured status.[12] Many Roman emperors attained the throne not by biological sonship but through adoption by the previous emperor.[13] Paul uses this image in Romans 8:12-17 to describe the new relationship a believer can have with God through Christ.

The household consisted also of friends and clients who might be freedpersons or others whose association was valuable to the household. To be a friend or client meant much more than we usually mean today. For instance, a slave who was to be set free but who chose to remain with his master could enter into a new relationship. That slave would promise loyalty to the interests of the household. The master would guarantee to provide for the material and social needs of the ex-slave and his family.[14]

In such a household structure, people of various social classes interacted with each other, just as they did on the large cotton and tobacco plantations of the American South in the eighteenth and nineteenth centuries. Yet the household could only survive as long as all members knew their place in the hierarchy and performed those tasks and obligations rel-

---

11. Everett Ferguson, *Backgrounds of Early Christianity* (Grand Rapids: Eerdmans, 1987), 54.

12. Tidball, *The Social Context of the New Testament*, 80.

13. For example, Julius Caesar adopted Augustus, Augustus adopted Tiberius, Tiberius adopted Germanicus (who died before he reached the throne). Four emperors of the second century who had no sons each adopted an heir to succeed them.

14. Tidball, *The Social Context of the New Testament*, 80.

ative to their status. Because of these wide gaps in social status, households were held together by economic interests, and often by a common religion. Such religion was chosen by the head of the household.[15]

Working for a Living: Occupations in Rome

As noted, the upper classes in the Roman Empire did not work for a living. Inherited wealth, property rentals, and money lent at high interest protected the rich from labor, which they felt was messy, demeaning, and often immoral. Work kept one from cultural and educational pursuits, from public life and friendships.[16] But our profiles of the five house churches and returning refugees show that all except Prisca likely had to work. What kind of work did they engage in, and how did it fit into the structures of their households? Were they proud of their work, or did it sap their energy and grind down their spirits?

We do not know much about how lower-class people felt about their work. Only powerful upper-class men had the educational skills and leisure to write. Since they saw slaves and other lower-class people existing merely for their benefit, they had no interest in understanding life "from below." One way of obtaining information is through inscriptions, most of them funeral epitaphs. These record more accurately than upper-class literature what was the actual lived reality of the person who had died, either in their own words or of someone close to them in life. But these inscriptions do not present a completely accurate picture either, for the poorest of the poor could not afford a funeral epitaph, and the majority of those who could afford it do not mention their occupation.

Sandra R. Joshel studied all the 6,167 Roman epitaphs discovered from this time period.[17] About one-sixth of them mention an occupation,

---

15. Tidball, *The Social Context of the New Testament,* 81.

16. Alison Burford, *Craftsmen in Greek and Roman Society* (London: Thames and London, 1972), 29.

17. Sandra R. Joshel, *Work, Identity, and Legal Status at Rome: A Study of the Occupational Inscriptions,* Oklahoma Series in Classical Culture (Norman and London: University of Oklahoma Press, 1992).

which means that at least for this minority, they had enough pride in their work to include a reference on their epitaph. Surprisingly, a much higher proportion of slaves and freedpersons mention an occupation than do freeborn persons, even though most of the latter would definitely have had to work for a living.[18]

Earlier interpreters thought these epitaphs showed that freedpersons and slaves dominated commerce and the trades. But Joshel believes that more men and women of slave origin included their occupation on their inscription because the work was so significant for them.[19] Their family ties would have been far weaker, since they never had a homeland and family of origin or it had been snatched away from them. Further, slaves could not legally marry; their children were not legally their own but belonged to the master. Slave families, if kept together at all, could be torn apart at any time.[20] The law viewed them as possessions of another. The only thing truly their own was their labor and the skills they had acquired at such labor.

The inscriptions list a wide range of occupations performed by working-class people in Rome. Joshel has organized the occupations into nine categories (classified by dominant function) and listed the number of inscriptions named in each category. They are: construction (112); manufacture (331); sales (108); banking (42); educated service (such as architects, doctors, midwives, and teachers: 120); skilled service (such as entertainers and hairdressers: 75); domestic service (321); transportation (55); and administrators, finance, and secretarial service (306).[21]

Looking at each of our Christian cell groups in Rome, what can we infer about the type of work the members are doing? Following are suggestions which can be used for the simulation. More imaginative details will be provided in a following chapter.

18. Exact statistics are available in Joshel, *Work, Identity, and Legal Status,* 47.

19. Joshel, 49.

20. Keith Bradley, *Slaves and Masters in the Roman Empire: A Study in Social Control,* Collection Latomus, vol. 185 (Bruxelles: Revue d'études Latines, 1984), 32.

21. Joshel, *Work, Identity, and Legal Status,* 174-176.

Establishing Household Structures

For the house-church simulation, take time to think through in more detail how each member relates to the others by (1) occupation and (2) social status.

The church that meets in the house of Prisca and Aquila (16:4-5) is the only example in Romans 16 where heads of a household are Christian and where others in their care or under their household authority are also apparently Christian. In this household some members are probably slaves, some freedpersons. Perhaps some free citizens are also attached to the household for economic reasons. Many will be engaged in Prisca and Aquila's tentmaking (or awning) business as male or female awning makers, weavers, or salespersons. A chief steward handles general management of the estate; a chief housekeeper works under him. Workers are always needed for spinning, making clothes, and laundry. As a noblewoman, Prisca (perhaps also Aquila) has the leisure for study, teaching the gospel, and perhaps preaching (see Acts 18:26).

How do such members of a hierarchical structure relate to each other when they have all been called equally into the grace of God? How might Prisca and Aquila's leadership be different from that in pagan households?

In the *households of Aristobulus and Narcissus* (16:10-11), men are likely to work in administration, finance, and secretarial services, although cooks, waiters, gardeners, construction workers, and teachers are needed in such large households. Women can be clerks, secretaries, ladies' maids, clothes folders, hairdressers, haircutters, readers, entertainers, midwives, and infirmary attendants. They will be working with other people who are not Christians.

If *the brothers* (16:14) and *the saints* (16:15) are located in the slum areas of Trastevere and Porta Capena, the members can choose from a wide range of trades and unskilled labor. Possibly each of these cell groups works together at some trade, women and men. Trastevere housed harbor workers, warehouse laborers, seamen, brick and tile workers, potters, millers, tanners and leatherworkers, fisher folk, and grain mill workers. Porta Capena was populated by traders; transport workers; dealers in cattle, slaves, marble, tanned hides, oil, wines; and all manner of artisans — ironsmiths, tinsmiths, coppersmiths, goldsmiths, painters, silkworkers, clothmakers, shoemakers, and others.

Tiny shops sell a variety of luxury goods or necessities. The shops and warehouses where these people work are on the ground floor of large tenement buildings. The workers live in tiny rooms on the upper floors. Perhaps some or all of them work for one master whose family lives in larger rooms on the second floor of a tenement.

Returning Jewish refugees may not yet have a sponsor, patron, or household to which they belong. How could they arrange to ply their trade without being part of the structure of a larger household and having a sponsor or patron? How might the Gentiles and resident Jews be able to help these former leaders who are now displaced refugees?

The *Koinōnia*

Although the household provided economic and social security for members of the Roman Empire, there was another structure which met deeper, emotional needs — unofficial voluntary associations, or clubs. People would gather with a common interest — a social or philanthropic cause, a trade, a philosophy, a religion. There were funerary associations, where members would pay certain fees to ensure that surviving members would pay their funeral expenses.

These voluntary associations met the need to *belong*. Some were not explicitly religious, but all had a religious dimension, such as an initiation ceremony, a ritual bath, or other purification rite — often with secrecy and preceded by fasting.[22] The new Christian religion benefited greatly from this model. First, it had come under the umbrella of Judaism, already viewed by the Romans as a voluntary association — even international in scope — and therefore recognized. Thus Christianity gained much headway throughout the Empire. Only when the church threatened the peace of the Empire did it come under scrutiny.[23]

22. Tidball, *The Social Context of the New Testament*, 87.
23. Tidball, *The Social Context of the New Testament*, 87-88.

Second, the concept of radical equality in the Christian gospel was more like the structure of the egalitarian clubs than the hierarchical household structure. But many clubs were only egalitarian to those members who could afford the initiation fees. This already discriminated between rich and poor. The Christian cell groups did not charge initiation fees; they were open to everyone.

The Roman government expressed little concern about these clubs and secret societies unless their meetings posed a threat to security. The recipients of Paul's letter to Rome were well aware that the Jewish voluntary association had been in recent trouble with the emperor Claudius. Seven or eight years earlier, he had expelled most of the Jews from Rome. So these house churches always had to keep an eye cocked toward the political scene.

The Roman house churches existed on the tension between *oikonomia* and *koinōnia*. Meeting in homes, they could not survive without the household structure to provide for economic and physical needs. At the same time, these groups met deeper emotional and spiritual needs than could the household. Even better, in *koinōnia* hierarchy was wiped away and all came to God in the same way — not through wealth or status or good works, but by responding to God's grace expressed in Jesus Christ.

Establishing Roles in Koinōnia *Structure*

For the house-church simulation, you now may visualize the character you are developing as a member of the body of Christ and think through your specific spiritual gifts. Each of you brings your own strengths and weaknesses to the house church. Each comes from a perspective as conservative, liberal, or somewhere in between.

Turn to Romans 12–14 and look for descriptions of spiritual gifts or moral strengths or weaknesses. Round out your personality and character by using clues from this passage. For example, a Jewish person or someone tending to be moralistic or conservative may be more inclined to keep the Law and not engage in drunkenness (13:13), but may also be less inclined to do acts of mercy toward Gentiles (12:7) or may want to take vengeance on those who have exiled or persecuted Jews — and thus get into political trouble (12:17–13:7).

On the other hand, a Gentile or one tending to be liberal may have more problems with drunkenness and quarreling but may also be more generous and hospitable. Remember that being a Jew does not necessarily make one conservative; some Jews may be reacting against their background and want to throw off the Law completely. Or a Gentile may have originally been attracted to Judaism because of its distinctive laws and claims, and thus prefer the security of keeping the Jewish Law.

Two particular items arise in chapter 14 — what to eat and what holy days to observe. Here the "weak" refers to the conservatives with a conscience against eating meat, while the "strong," more liberal, eat anything. Conservatives carefully kept the Sabbath and many other holy days, while liberals thought that the holy days of Jewish tradition were not necessary for them to observe. (Romans 12–15 will be studied in more detail in chapters 10–11.)

Now write your personal information for the character sketch on page 24 or appendix 3, number 1.

5 | Isis, Mithras, or Stoicism:
Religions and Philosophies in Rome

The first time I led a simulation on Romans, people developing their characters would ask, "How would I have heard about Jesus? What would have made me decide to become a Christian instead of belonging to another religion?"

To answer them, we must take a broader look at the religious scene in first-century Rome. When the gospel of Jesus Christ arrived there some years earlier, the stage was already crowded with religions. No strong anti-religious feeling existed. In some ways the religious environment was similar to that of North America today, where we are proud of our religious freedom and diversity. In the United States we have broadly based civil religion represented by "In God We Trust" on pennies and by speeches on the Fourth of July about the faith and wisdom of founding forefathers. Politicians frequently proclaim their religious affinities to gain support from constituents or in conjunction with values they want to promote.

In addition, many other religions or variations of Christianity are available, depending on private choice and personal opinion. Limitations are only placed on practices which interfere with others' freedom or which defy the law or public morality.

Such variety also existed in Rome, but with significant differences. For one, our Judeo-Christian heritage has influenced most people today to assume the existence of only one God, good and all powerful. It was not so in Rome. Though monotheism sometimes emerged in the form of the Great Mother, the Sky-Father, or the Sun-God, it was always in tension with polytheism. Polytheism in Rome meant that a person could belong to more than one religion, worship a variety of deities, and participate in as many religious rites as one could afford. Since pagans believed the gods ruled the cosmos and could help or harm them, it was necessary for them to pay their respects to as many as possible. One could never be too careful.

A second difference between ancient Rome and later Western religious assumptions is that, except in Judaism, ethical behavior was not necessarily related to religious practice. It was the philosophers, not the priests, who taught ethics. Though the gods were more powerful than humans, they were amoral.

Following are a few of the choices available to first-century Romans:

The Roman Pantheon

More than anything else, the poetry of Homer in the *Iliad* and the *Odyssey* around 700 B.C. had shaped the picture of the Greek pantheon, with Zeus as father and the subordinate gods and goddesses assuming specialized functions. Hera was guardian of marriage, Hermes the messenger of the gods. Poseidon's realm was the sea. Artemis protected wild nature and animals. Ares presided over war, with Athena a wise warrior-maid and patron of craftsmen. Aphrodite was goddess of love; Hephaestus was the god of fire, of smiths, and of technology.

Later, Roman contact with Greeks led to the assimilation of the Greek and Roman pantheons, with Zeus metamorphosing into Jupiter, Hera into Juno, Ares into Mars, Athena into Minerva, Artemis into Diana, Aphrodite into Venus, Poseidon into Neptune, Hephaestus into Volcanus, and Hermes into Mercury.[1]

By the end of the Roman Republic in 44 B.C., this traditional religion had fallen into neglect. But Augustus, who ruled as the first emperor (27 B.C.-A.D. 14), set about to rebuild shrines and renew religion. As a shrewd politician, he saw the value of promoting civil religion to unify the Empire and strengthen his position as a benefactor of religion.[2] His successors followed this policy.

1. John Ferguson, *The Religions of the Roman Empire* (Ithaca, N.Y.: Cornell University Press, 1970), 70-71.
2. Cary and Scullard, *A History of Rome,* 341-342.

Worship of the Roman pantheon was primarily observed by the upper classes, who wielded most of the political power. They kept the traditions as symbolic of a comfortable, familiar way of life. As the Senate received more and more members from outlying provinces, local gods came along. They would merge into the Roman pantheon; thus Isis could be the same as Venus or perhaps another goddess. New gods were also added to the pantheon in the form of previous emperors.

The Cult of the Emperor

In Egypt divine kingship was a long-established practice. Among the Greeks, Alexander the Great set a new standard when in 324 B.C. he demanded that people recognize his deity. Later Hellenistic rulers called themselves divine by using titles of "Savior" and "Benefactor."[3] In Luke 22:25-26, Jesus says, "The kings of the Gentiles lord it over them; and those in authority over them are called benefactors. But not so with you." John's Gospel understands this practice by calling Jesus "Savior."

The model of divine kingship was adopted to some extent by ambitious Roman rulers. Augustus and most emperors who followed him did not directly declare themselves gods, although Augustus allowed temples to be built to himself — so long as his name was coupled with Roma, the spirit of Rome. Tiberius, who followed him, was also cautious and did not accept deification, though he was given such after his death. He was followed by "Mad" Caligula, who demanded worship as a god. Claudius, who had ruled during the lifetimes of all the Roman Christians whom Paul addressed (A.D. 41-54) had, like Tiberius, not asked for divine honors. But he did not refuse them and after death was accorded divinity. Nero, the present emperor, was openly courting such worship.

This worship was a civic duty, not spiritual. Its purpose was to inspire awe toward the emperor and to maintain the unity and hegemony of the Empire. It expressed one's submission to the state in the guise of religious ritual (somewhat like God-and-country flag wavers today).

3. John Ferguson, *The Religions of the Roman Empire*, 89.

Personal Religion — The Mysteries

The state religion did not satisfy emotional and religious needs of individuals. For that, many turned to the mysteries, which came in from the East and were quite popular among immigrants in Rome. Numerous mystery shrines have been excavated in the Porta Capena and Trastevere areas of Rome.[4] In this case, the word *mystery* refers not to *mysticism* but to voluntary, secret, and personal initiations involved in a particular cult. The goal was to have a mind-changing experience of the sacred.[5] The mysteries were diverse, but John Ferguson notes that they have three common features: (1) a ritual of purification through which the initiate has to pass, (2) communion with some god or goddess, and (3) the promise of an afterlife of bliss for the faithful.[6] Walter Burkert sees little emphasis on resurrection symbolism and more on good luck and a long life here and now.[7]

Of the many mysteries in first-century Rome, five are described below:

- *Eleusis.* This cult was based on the myth of Demeter searching for her daughter Kore (KŌ-ray) (Persephone), whom Hades carried off to the underworld and who returned for part of each year. Originally located in Athens, it had flourished since the sixth century B.C.
- *Dionysus,* or Bacchus, was the god of wine and ecstasy, the phallus being his symbol. However, there was no local center, so great variations of the cult existed. In earlier times membership seems to have been restricted to women who several times a year would leave their families and rigid sex roles to perform ecstatic rites in the countryside.[8] During first-century Rome, there were many Dionysian clubs, usually dependent on a wealthy founder. Initiations were so secret

4. Lampe, *Die stadtrömischen Christen,* 42.

5. Walter Burkert, *Ancient Mystery Cults* (Cambridge, Mass.: Harvard University Press, 1987), 11.

6. John Ferguson, *The Religions of the Roman Empire,* 99.

7. Burkert, *Ancient Mystery Cults,* 23-24.

8. Ross S. Kraemer, *Her Share of the Blessings: Women's Religions Among Pagans, Jews, and Christians in the Greco-Roman World* (New York, Oxford: Oxford University Press, 1992), 39-43.

that no one knows how the organization worked. However, by this time more men were involved, and much of the sexual debauchery associated with Dionysian worship was committed by men with other men and with young boys.[9]

- *The Mother Goddess* was also known as Magna Mater, Meter, or Kybele, and her cult can be traced back to the Stone Age. It was brought to Rome in 204 B.C. because an oracle said the Mother would make Rome victorious in its war with Hannibal. In the myth, Attis, lover of the Mother, is castrated and dies under a pine tree. In imitation, the priests of the cult castrated themselves and became eunuchs. Various forms of the rites existed, but the most spectacular was the *taurobolium:* the initiate, crouching in a pit covered with wooden beams over which a bull was slaughtered, was drenched in the bull's blood.

- *Isis* was an Egyptian goddess. In the myth, she searches for Osiris, her murdered, dismembered husband. Isis finds and reassembles him, conceives by him, and gives birth to Horus. The big temple of Isis in Rome had been recently founded by Caligula (A.D. 37-41). Isis and Osiris were often identified with Demeter and Dionysus.

  Both women and men joined the cult of Isis, and some degree of egalitarianism existed, although it would have been hard for poor persons to pay the initiation fees. Women held many offices in the cult. Isis protected marital fidelity and emphasized the nuclear family. In this respect, Isis worship directly related to the realities of many women's lives.[10]

- *Mithras* was an old Indo-Iranian deity, known from the Bronze Age onward. The cult met in subterranean grottoes, where small groups of men met for initiations and for sacrificial meals in front of a painting or relief of Mithras slaying the bull. There were seven grades of initiation. Only men were permitted, and the cult was popular among soldiers, merchants, and officials of the Empire. The *taurobolium* was also used. Ritual meals were lavish, which indicates the poor were not welcome.

---

9. Kraemer, *Her Share of the Blessings,* 45.
10. Kraemer, *Her Share of the Blessings,* 74-78.

More information on the mysteries will be included in chapter 6, when we study Romans 5–6.

Philosophies

The philosophers of the Greco-Roman age taught people to live in a hostile world with self-sufficiency, which often meant nonattachment. Two well-known philosophies of first-century Rome were Epicureanism and Stoicism.

- *Epicureanism* was critical of conventional religion and superstition and appeared to reject them on rational grounds. Epicureans did believe in the gods but felt that they were unconcerned with the world and would neither reward nor punish. The soul was not immortal. The aim of life was pleasure, not in the hedonistic surface sense, but through cultivating friendships and avoiding pain. Thus ideally Epicureanism renounced worldly ambition and pursuit of wealth, power, and fame. Peace of mind was attained by controlling desire and eliminating fear — the main fears being fear of the gods and fear of death.[11]
- *Stoicism.* The Stoics were pantheists. They had five arguments for the existence of God, who was the totality of all things seen and unseen: (1) humankind agrees that god exists, (2) someone has to be the highest in a scale of being, (3) a principle has to unify the universe, (4) the order in nature implies an ordering mind, and (5) piety, holiness, and wisdom imply the existence of god as their object.[12] Unlike Christianity, the Stoics believed that each soul was a spark of the divine and after death the soul would retain its individuality for a time but eventually be absorbed into the divine fire.[13]

11. John Ferguson, *The Religions of the Roman Empire*, 190-193.
12. John Ferguson, *The Religions of the Roman Empire*, 193.
13. John Ferguson, *The Religions of the Roman Empire*, 194.

The Stoics preached acceptance of one's state in life, be it slave or senator. Virtue lay in the attitude of the soul, not in action.[14] Unfortunately, this made their philosophy seem indifferent to the pain in the world, and thus static and unrevolutionary.

Judaism

Judaism was a distinct and exclusive religion. There was only one God, Yahweh, and no other could be worshiped. Jews had sacred writings that gave them a history going back over a thousand years — or to the beginning of creation. Unlike other religions, Judaism had a strong ethical emphasis derived from the Bible. Besides the Ten Commandments, Jews adhered to other Mosaic laws, circumcising males (who were often valued more highly than females), observing the Sabbath, and heeding dietary restrictions.

Because of their distinctiveness, Jews had an uncertain status in the culture. Sometimes they were awarded special political privileges, such as exemption from military conscription. At other times they were discriminated against. Judaism's special appeal to Gentiles lay in its emphasis on the holiness of one God and on ethical living.

Choosing Christ

We will now return to our question of how the early Roman Christians made their choice for Christ. We know how Jews became Christians, since Christ Jesus was proclaimed as the fulfillment of the messianic hope recorded in their prophetic writings (*christos* is Greek for *the Anointed One, Messiah*). We also know from the book of Acts that when Paul and his companions were rejected by Jews in a particular city, they would preach to the Gentiles.

No doubt many of these Gentiles are those who were previously attracted to Judaism — perhaps because of their desires for moral standards

14. John Ferguson. *The Religions of the Roman Empire*, 194.

and for a relationship with one exclusive, holy, omnipotent God. These Gentiles would likely already be associating with a Jewish synagogue and keeping at least some of the Mosaic laws. More Gentile women than men seem to have been attracted to Judaism (such as Lydia in Acts 16), perhaps because circumcision was not an issue for them. Yet Judaism did not educate its women in the Law as it did men.[15] Now the message was proclaimed that Yahweh God equally accepts all who believe in God's Son, Christ Jesus, without circumcision and regardless of gender. Perhaps it was easier for these devout Gentiles to embrace the new faith than for circumcised Jews.

But Christianity was spreading beyond Gentiles with Jewish sympathies. Why? What was its appeal?

- First was the person of its founder, Jesus Christ. Stories of his life, teachings, healings, death, resurrection, and ascension were told and retold. His Spirit had come upon the early believers and was still available for those who believed and were baptized. His presence was known during the sharing of bread and wine in the Eucharist. Paul's own life had been totally turned around since his encounter with the risen Jesus.
- Second was the way of love revealed through the Christian communities (*koinōnia*). In these communities everyone was accepted — Jew and Gentile, slave and free, women and men — on the same footing. This was quite novel in the status-conscious, male-dominated Greco-Roman world. Slaves and other poor were often barred from mystery initiations because of the fees. Mithras did not admit women, while even the cult of Isis required a male as high priest.

In Christianity, women were not only accepted, but many became leaders, as we have seen through the names of Romans 16. The poor and needy were cared for, the babies thrown out to die were rescued and raised. Even the pagan Celsus, writing an indictment against Christianity in the second century, declared that "where other

15. Tidball, *The Social Context of the New Testament*, 85.

mystery-religions invite the pure and righteous, Christians invite crooks and simpletons, yes, and women and children, and the very teachers are wool-workers and cobblers and laundry-workers."[16] Indeed, our concept of universal democracy seems to have originated in early Christianity.

- Third was the strength of conviction that cut through the multitude of religious choices offered in the ancient world. The reality of the Spirit's presence now and the certainty of the resurrection of the body and the coming reign of Christ contrasted strongly with the vague hints of future bliss promised by the mysteries. Such good news enabled many to endure persecution and martyrdom without flinching, which in turn attracted others to the faith.
- Fourth was the ethical emphasis taken over from Judaism and which ultimately proceeded from the practice of agape love.
- On the practical level, it would not have been hard for the Christian message to spread in a city where most people lived outdoors and rubbed shoulders on streets, at the baths, and in their shops and packed tenement houses. In 2 Thessalonians 3:8, Paul speaks of laboring night and day so he would not be a burden to the believers there. Likely he worked in a shop with other tentmakers or leatherworkers, making his living while he taught others about salvation through Jesus. In the same way, the gospel could have easily spread to Gentiles unconnected to Jewish synagogues in Rome, simply by workers sharing good news with each other on the job.

*   *   *

If you are developing your character for a simulation, think through and record on your character sketch (pages 24 or 184-85) how you would have heard the message about Christ and become a Christian.

16. John Ferguson, *The Religions of the Roman Empire*, 127.

6 | Creating Characters and Reconstructing House Churches

In this chapter we move back almost 2,000 years to the spring of 57, when Phoebe delivered and proclaimed Paul's letter to the Roman Christians.

Now you may review your character sketch and share who you are with other members of your house-church group, even if you are still uncertain about some details. It would be good to work out a balance of diversity with other members of your group. Once when I taught Romans, we developed characters this way:

The House Church of Prisca and Aquila

Prisca is the primary leader who convenes the discussion. She has many skills in reading and teaching, since she attended school as a child in a noble Roman family. She generally supports Paul's outlook and comes across as a woman of even-handedness and wisdom. She often speaks of past experiences she and Aquila have had with Paul and helps to explain some of his personality "quirks" and passion for sharing the gospel.

Aquila, her husband, from a Jewish background, better understands and appreciates some of Paul's concerns to maintain continuity with Jewish history. He is perhaps more sympathetic to those who want to keep the Jewish laws than Paul himself is. He supervises the leatherworking-awning business, which partially supports the household.

Felicia serves as manager of the day-to-day activities of the household, planning meals and supervising cloth making. She is non-Jewish and feels that the Jewish Law is of little importance for herself, but she makes some effort to shop for foods that Jewish members of the household can eat without a guilty conscience.

Olympius represents the most liberal perspective. As a Gentile member of the household who often takes trips to obtain or sell awnings for the household business, he is a man of the world. He has been converted through stories of the miracles of Jesus and by the power shown in God raising him from the dead. That sounded more impressive to him than tales of the old Roman gods and goddesses. He sees no reason for anyone keeping the Jewish laws — although he always appreciates a chance to rest on the Sabbath when in Jewish company!

Aurelia is a young Gentile slave with no biological family connections. As an infant, she was exposed by unknown parents who did not want another girl, and was rescued and raised as a slave in this household. She is a weaver for Aquila's awning business. But she has also taught herself to read and write and shows definite signs of leadership ability. She has a good grasp of the gospel and is able to follow Paul's line of argument. Aurelia is struggling with the tension between her status as slave and the egalitarian claims of the gospel.

Epaenetus (ep-a-NEET-us) is Jewish, an acquaintance of Prisca and Aquila who was expelled from Rome eight years earlier. His instincts are conservative; keeping the Jewish holy days and dietary laws are important to him. By profession he is a butcher and knows how to prepare meat and other foods so they are kosher for Jews. He wants to become part of this house church, both spiritually and economically, as the household's butcher. Felicia is suspicious of Epaenetus because he poses a threat to the way she handles the management of food and cooking in the household. One of the running questions throughout the study of the Romans letter becomes whether or not Epaenetus should join this household and this house church.

Theotekna (thee-o-TEK-na) is a Gentile slave from another household who has become friends with Aurelia through association at the local market and well. Through Aurelia she embraced the gospel and is attending the daily worship and eucharistic services in the household of Prisca and Aquila — whenever she can take time off. Her master is not Christian and can be physically and verbally abusive. Several times he raped her — his legal right as a slaveowner.

I have also composed partial character sketches for members of other house churches:

Those of the Household of Aristobulus

Eutuchas (U-tu-kas) is an accountant and an assistant to the head administrator of this household. He is well-trained in business and keeps the books on the household's vineyards in northern Italy, where slaves and tenant freedpersons work on a large farm. His Jewish parents were slaves freed in their later years, but he was born while they were still in slavery, so he is a slave. He is circumcised and keeps the Jewish Law as much as possible. He heard of Jesus through Aquila, a client of his master. He is anti-Zealot and sees Jesus Christ as Messiah in a spiritual sense. Eutuchas has a bright future as a highly trained bureaucrat and is conflicted about whether Judea should have its own government free from Rome.

Kalandria is a slave in a long-term relationship with Eutuchas. They are not legally married, since slave marriages are not officially recognized. They have two living children, now teenagers. One son died at the age of 3. The master granted them the privilege of keeping and raising their children. Kalandria is a hairdresser and attendant for the mistress and her daughters. They are vain and fussy, often verbally abusing her for not combing their hair right. Kalandria was exposed as an infant, found, and raised by a poor family who sold her to a slavetrader when she was 12. Since then she has been with this household. She observes Jewish religious practices because Eutuchas is Jewish and she heard of Christ through him.

Seleucus (sel-LUKE-as), 19, is a waiter at private meals of the master and his family, and for public meals with many guests. Newly captured from Parthia in the East, he speaks only Greek. He is homesick without his family, who were all initiates into the Isis cult. Eutuchas and Kalandria have introduced him to Christianity and are teaching him to read and count in his spare time. He is quickly learning about the Scriptures. The head waiter, also a slave, is perfectionistic and sometimes verbally and physically abusive to Seleucus. Seleucus does not see the Jewish Law as very important.

Herodes (her-ROAD-es) is the teacher of the master's children and the children of two important clients. The students are all aged between 10 and 15. As a slave in this household, he is bright, gets along well with children, and was trained in Greek, Latin, and Roman history and geography. He is Jewish and knows Jewish history well, but does not tell superiors he's Jewish. Previously he dabbled in Mithraism but was never initiated. It was too expensive, and he was too much of a Jew to embrace any other religion. He also heard of Christ from Eutuchas.

Gaia (GĪ-a) is a Greek slave, the "wife" of Herodes, and an assistant cook who also purchases food at the market. Her memory is phenomenal, and she is good at numbers and loves to bargain with the foodsellers. But she only reads at a functional level. Gaia grew up as a slave in this household and has natural leadership skills. She and Herodes had one living child sold away from them at the age of 10. Gaia had an early interest in the Mother mysteries, but was never initiated because she couldn't pay the fee. She was happy with Judaism, which she observed with Herodes, but has since been baptized as a Christian through the witness of Eutuchas and Kalandria.

Isidoros (ice-i-DOOR-os), a Greek and slaveborn, is secretary for the household head. He keeps track of his schedule, writes letters, and accompanies him to important meetings to take notes. Proficient in Greek and Latin, he hopes for manumission later. He has a sensitive conscience and was attracted to Judaism because of its ethical system and now has converted to the Christian faith through other members of the cell group.

Daphne, a dressmaker and weaver, was freed only three years ago. Since then she still sometimes sews for her previous mistress and her daughters for a small salary, as well as for the mistress's acquaintances. She is a Greek-speaking Jew brought to Rome twenty-five years earlier and sold to this household. She had three children in a long-term relationship with the slave Athenion, but he and two of the children were sold fifteen years ago. She has met for Sabbath worship with other Jewish slaves for years and was converted to Christ through Kalandria.

Herodion (he-ROAD-i-on) is a Jewish Christian freeman who used to be a leader of this cell group, but who was expelled in 49. He met Paul in Asia and accepted his ideas on freedom from the Jewish Law. Now he is returning and wants to be received back into his house church. But there are strong divisions of opinion about whether or not everyone should keep the Jewish Law. Herodion is trained as a scribe, but naturally lost his job in this household when he was exiled. He would like to get his position back.

Those of the Household of Narcissus

Aelia (AY-li-a) and *Caulius* are a slave couple who are chief housekeeper and chief steward for the household. They have been together for fifteen years and have three living children. In 49, when Claudius issued the edict expelling Jews, Aelia and Caulius inquired about "Chrestus," since they, as chief administrators, had contact among the Jewish craftsmen in Trastevere. They were converted to Christ in 50 and began a group in their household. They kept this secret from Narcissus and now from Nero and the present head of the household.

Zonius is an accountant and bookkeeper for the household. He loves numbers and is an efficient slave. He was attracted to Christianity by the love expressed among the cell group and by the stories of Jesus. His former religion was Mithraism, and the hardest thing about becoming a Christian for him was to accept pacifism and the idea of loving one's enemies. Zonius wants his freedom and the chance to make his own living, so he is working hard to favorably impress the household head.

Diana, 20, was exposed at birth and raised by people who sold her to the household of Narcissus at age 11. A slave, she is ladies' maid to the mistress and her daughters and helps them dress, tidies up the room, holds the mirror, walks with their litter when they travel, and helps them in and out. At 18, she was repeatedly raped by a slave in the household and had a child at 19. However, it was taken away from her to be raised by slaves elsewhere. Aelia told her about Jesus Christ. The cell group meets some of Diana's need for love and prays with her for her baby girl.

Europus is a Greek-speaking slave taken from his homeland at 14 and thus without a family. He is "married" to another slave in the household, but she is not a Christian. He is a scribe and secretary, having been trained to read and write. Europus is interested in philosophy and has been a Stoic, but now he prefers a more personal God as expressed through Jesus Christ.

Guadentius (gaw-DEN-shi-ous) and *Gesatia* (ge-SATi-a) are a freed couple in a client relationship with the household. Gaudentius is administrator of an imperial estate in Macedonia, farmed by a paid steward. He travels there several times a year. Although Jewish, he did not observe traditions until he joined Jews in Thessalonica (in the province of Macedonia). After Paul visited there, he heard of Christ through the Christians in the Thessalonian church and was converted. Every time Gaudentius travels, he brings back more stories about Jesus and the spread of the Christian faith in Macedonia. Gesatia had a rather liberal Egyptian Jewish background and is well-read. She does a lot of weaving and sewing for the household, as well as providing spiritual leadership. She and Gaudentius have two children in their late teens who are also part of the cell group.

Tryphaena and *Tryphosa* are Jewish sisters who were independent freed saleswomen before being expelled from Rome. They moved to Phillipi and eventually met Lydia (Acts 16) after her conversion to Christianity. They joined her business of producing and selling purple cloth. Now they want to establish a business in Rome and use it as a way to evangelize. They are seeking a patron in the household of Narcissus and would like to join the Christian cell group for worship. But they are disturbed by how little the Scriptures are read and studied by the Narcissiani, and they would like to begin a teaching ministry there. Will the Narcissiani accept them, or think they are too critical or bossy?

Housing: Persons in cell groups in both the households of Aristobulus and Narcissus have small rooms in tenements adjoining the villas.

The Brothers and Sisters

Most of the Brothers and Sisters are cobblers who live in small rooms in an *insula,* or tenement house, in Porta Capena. They work together in a shop on the first floor. Most are freedpersons who live at a subsistence level. *Hermes* and *Patrobas* are shoe salesmen who travel from door to door or sit in the marketplace with their wares.

Phlegon (FLEH-gon) and *Dorea* are in charge of the shop. They were both freed five years ago but still owe deference to their former owner, who lives six blocks away. They must visit him each morning and in exchange he finds some customers for their shoes. Phlegon and Dorea became Christians in the household where they had worked as slaves alongside a Christian Jew. They were attracted to Judaism's monotheism and ethics and are learning to read the Greek Scriptures (Septuagint). *Suria* (SUR-i-a), their teenage daughter, takes care of the young children of the shoemakers.

Hermas is a young slave-apprentice of Phlegon who is learning the cobbler's trade. *Irene* is a doctor-midwife, a freedwoman who learned medicine as a slave and who now works mostly with lower-class people. She is the wife of *Asyncritus* and the daughter of Greek slaves but does not know anything about her parents because she was sold away from them as a young child. Before becoming believers, Hermas followed the Eleusinian mysteries, and Irene those of Isis.

Chrysas (CRY-sas) is a new Christian, a young woman living in the same tenements, who was exposed and raised as a slave. She is a friend of Suria and a seamstress and clothes mender for a family of tinsmiths two blocks away. Formerly she was an adherent of Isis.

Persis and her husband, Stephanus, have been co-leaders of this group with Phlegon and Dorea. Because of their ties with a nearby Jewish synagogue, they were expelled from Rome in 49, traveled east, and met Paul in Corinth, where Stephanus died. Now Persis has returned to rejoin both the shoemaker's trade and the cell group. Persis is a warm and loving middle-aged woman and a natural leader (Paul calls her "the beloved"). Yet the group is nervous about her return. They want to avoid any political trouble or loss of their shop. Life is precarious as it is. Some of them worry about Paul's influence on Persis. The conservatives among them think Paul is too liberal, and the liberals think he's too conservative. With Paul's letter coming, tension has increased.

The Saints

The Saints, who live in a tenement in Trastevere (Tras-TEV-e-ra), are weavers and dyers. Like the Brothers and Sisters, their shop is on the first floor and their living quarters in upper floors. It is always a struggle to pay the rent every month, and the tenement is so poorly constructed that the walls tend to crumble.

Philologus (fil-LOLL-o-gus), the head dyer, is not the owner of the factory. As a freedman, he learned this trade on the job. He and *Julia*, his wife, became leaders in this group after the more openly known Jewish leaders were exiled in 49. Julia, freeborn as the daughter of freedpersons, is in charge of the weaving.

Nereus (NEAR-e-us) and his sister *Rebecca* were sold together and left their Jewish parents at the ages of 8 and 10. They were bought by the owner of the factory and are now 23 and 25. Nereus, a weaver, keeps the books as an accountant and is "married" to *Posilla*, a spinner. Rebecca is a childcare worker for the master's children and also teaches the children in the synagogue. She is "married" to *Philippus* (fil-LEAP-us), a salesman on the street. He is a freedman and client to his former master, who provides buyers for the cloth.

Olympus and *Mara* are husband and wife, dyers who work with Philologus. Olympas is a freedman; Mara is freeborn. They have three children. This cell group, nearly all Jewish, heard about Jesus through the preaching of *Andronicus* and *Junia*, a Jewish couple who traveled to Jerusalem for Pentecost over twenty years ago, when the Holy Spirit came. Andronicus and Junia became believers and returned to Rome to preach the gospel as apostles of Jesus Christ. They were expelled in 49 and are now returning to their Christian cell group. How will they be received?

*   *   *

You will be developing nuances and personality quirks about your character as you go along. Various issues raised in Paul's letter will bring out different aspects of your character's personality. Do not be afraid to be a little more extreme (more conservative, liberal, outspoken, or outrageous) than you are in real life. Feel free to argue with Paul. What he wrote then was not yet considered Scripture, nor is he even the apostle who founded your church. Spicy discussion will remind us of how human and ordinary were those earliest Christian believers.

7 | Once upon a Time in a Faraway Land

We now leave our character sketches for a short time and look at another area of the study of Paul's letter to the Romans — rhetoric. Every literary work has its own style and structure so readers can understand it. When we hear "Once upon a time," we expect a fairy story or folktale. When we hear "It was a dark and stormy night," a Gothic romance comes to mind. If we start reading "August 6, 2006. Dear Mary, How are you?" we assume we will hear a personal letter.

What about Romans as a literary work? We know it is some kind of letter, created and dictated by Paul (1:1), written in Tertius's hand (16:22), directed to all of God's people in Rome (1:7), and carried there by Phoebe, a sister Christian (16:1-2). What else might the style and structure of the letter tell us about its meaning?

As we noted in chapter 1, more attention is usually paid to Romans as a theological or doctrinal treatise than as a letter written or as a speech delivered orally. One can check almost any commentary on Romans and find that authors compose their outlines by theological themes. If you have studied Romans in church school, the textbook you used probably did the same thing.

However, when we outline Romans by theological themes, we almost inevitably overlay it with our own theological presuppositions. In the 1500s Martin Luther was liberated by Romans because he read there a doctrine of justification by faith which met his psychological and spiritual needs. When he wrote his commentary, he centered it around this doctrine. Most later interpreters of Romans have been influenced by Luther and read through Luther's eyes. This can distort Paul's original theology and lead us to see the letter as an abstract thesis. Then we are cut off from the human situation we are simulating right now.

As Paul writes Romans, he does not tell us, with titles and headings, what outline he has in mind. The letter was written on scarce and precious parchment or papyrus, leaving no room for punctuation, paragraph indentation, headings, or margins. We must look elsewhere for clues.

Recently, scholars have begun looking at speaking and writing styles used in Greco-Roman culture. Educated people used careful structure in writing and public speaking. As a main course, schools taught rhetoric, the art of speech-making. People of the ancient world thought becoming a persuasive and powerful speaker was one of the greatest accomplishments.[1] In fact, rhetoric was taught and used to understand biblical texts until a century ago, when there was a definite move away from it.[2]

Today schools pay little attention to rhetoric. The word *rhetoric* is often used in a pejorative way. If a political speech is "just rhetoric," we mean it has well-polished words with little or no substance behind them.

Yet if we think of rhetoric as a way to structure a speech or production, our media-oriented culture uses it heavily. Every television program is shaped to fit within time limits, to be interrupted by commercial breaks, and to make one or two main points. One of my favorite TV shows used to be "Murder, She Wrote." I watched it enough to predict who will be murdered when, and about what time the sleuth, Jessica Fletcher, will get the flash of insight that helps her solve the mystery. I could usually count on the murderer's reaction and confession at the end.

What does all this have to do with Romans? Perhaps as our culture moves away from so much dependence on print toward visual and audio media, this may help us better appreciate Romans as an oral speech.

---

1. A good introduction is Burton L. Mack's *Rhetoric and the New Testament* (Minneapolis: Fortress, 1990), especially chapter 2, "The Classical Tradition as Cultural Context," 25-48.

2. Mack, *Rhetoric and the New Testament*, 12.

Three Important Speaking Styles

Scholars who study ancient rhetoric have identified three major rhetorical styles used by Greek and Roman orators:[3]

- *Deliberative.* Advice is offered by an authoritative figure to whom specific questions are posed or to whose attention problems are brought. Paul uses this style in 1 Thessalonians and 1 Corinthians.
- *Forensic.* This is a defense offered by an authoritative figure whose status has been threatened by competitors and accusers. A forensic style is used in Galatians; Paul strongly opposes those who emphasize the Jewish Law.
- *Demonstrative.* This style establishes a sense of community centered on values recognized by the audience. A contemporary example is a Fourth of July speech on American independence and ingenuity. Paul uses this style in Romans. Here he appeals to a particular value, the faith commitment of speaker and audience.

Roman teachers further classified speeches into subtypes. For demonstrative rhetoric alone, classics scholar Theodore Burgess has found twenty-seven subtypes. Robert Jewett identifies one of these as especially fitting for Romans — *the ambassador's speech.*

What characteristics of a political ambassador's introductory speech appear in Paul's speech to the Romans? In "Romans as an Ambassadorial Letter,"[4] Jewett notes a call for unity, good feelings between different nations, good will toward each other, values held in common, and the importance or power of the country or institution the ambassador represents.

---

3. George Kennedy, *New Testament Interpretation Through Rhetorical Criticism* (Chapel Hill and London: University of North Carolina Press, 1984), 19; Wilhelm Wuellner, "Paul's Rhetoric of Argumentation in Romans," in *The Romans Debate*, ed. Karl P. Donfried (Peabody, Mass.: Hendrickson, 1991), 139.

4. Robert Jewett, "Romans as an Ambassadorial Letter," *Interpretation* (1986): 382-389. Two alternate structures are suggested by Martin Luther Stirewalt, Jr., "The Form and Function of the Greek Letter-Essay," and David E. Aune, "Romans as a *Logos Protreptikos*," in *The Romans Debate*, 147-171, 278-296.

Check Paul's introduction in Romans 1:1-17. Notice the diplomacy he uses to appeal to *all* the Roman Christians and how he affirms the power of the "king" (God through Jesus Christ) whom he is representing.

Because of the work of scholars like Wilhelm Wuellner and Robert Jewett, we see the rhetorical structure of Romans and thus better understand Paul's purpose in writing. Paul wanted to bring together the diverse groups of Christians in Rome by appealing to shared faith in Christ. This was necessary preparation for his mission to Spain.

Phoebe and the Proclamation of Romans

Because Romans functions as a speech rather than a letter, Phoebe's role takes on new significance. She is not merely a postal carrier but the proclaimer and interpreter of Paul's speech. Phoebe will visit the different house churches, gathering together as many as possible in one place. She (or a professional rhetor brought along for the occasion) will read through the entire text in one sitting. Thus the listeners, accustomed to Roman rhetoric, will be able to follow the argument from beginning to end.

This is followed by group discussion and Phoebe's interpretation. As the leader of the church at Cenchreae and a co-worker with Paul, Phoebe understands Paul's mind and his particular emphases. She has heard him proclaim major parts of the speech before. This is an oral culture, and much explanation is left out of the writing and expounded orally. Phoebe is the ideal person to be an "ambassador for the ambassador" and clarify Paul's message.

Was Romans too long to read in one sitting? Not at all! In a culture without news sound bytes, half-hour TV shows, and fast-action video games, such an event was high entertainment. The text of Romans is shorter than either of the speeches Abraham Lincoln and Stephen Douglas gave at their debate of 1856, an event enthusiastically attended by thousands. In our post–Martin Luther King era, few of us appreciate the fine art of spoken rhetoric.

Because of the structure of our classes and because we are not used to listening to long speeches, this book breaks up Romans into its rhetorical parts. You will read or listen to one section at a time and discuss it. If you are in a class, "Phoebe" will proclaim it. Then members of each house church will discuss what they've heard and whether they can agree with it. Everyone will be encouraged and complimented, and everyone's toes will be stepped on!

Rhetorical Outline of Romans

This outline is simplified from that suggested by Robert Jewett in his essay, "Following the Argument of Romans."[5] It reflects rhetorical principles promoted by ancient handbooks. Cicero and Quintilian, both Latin rhetoricians, advise that a discourse be organized into six sections:

- Introduction
- Narration of the case
- Statement of the thesis
- Proof of the thesis
- Rebuttal of opposing views
- Conclusion

Romans, however, does not contain the fifth element, the rebuttal of opposing views. This would be included in a forensic discourse on a controversial issue; the speaker would argue for one position and against others (as in Galatians). As an ambassadorial letter, Romans is meant to encourage the attitude of listeners in a particular direction.

Leaving out the rebuttal, the other five rhetorical elements of Romans are found in these passages:

- *Introduction (1:1-7)*.
- *Narration (1:8-15)*. This gives the background of the missionary project as the reason to come to Rome.
- *Thesis Statement (1:16-17)*. The gospel is the powerful embodiment of

5. *The Romans Debate*, 265-277.

the righteousness of God. It is for both Jews and Gentiles, dependent only on God's grace and their faithful response to grace.

- *Proofs (1:18–15:13)*. Paul presents four proofs of his thesis statement: that the righteousness of God, rightly understood, can transform and unify the Roman house churches and their participation in world mission.

- *Conclusion (15:14–16:27)*. Paul appeals for cooperation among the Roman house churches on behalf of missionary activities in Rome, Jerusalem, and Spain.

For the *four proofs* (1:18–15:13) of his thesis statement, Paul follows the styles suggested by ancient rhetoric: those of confirmation and amplification:

1. *Confirmation (1:18–4:25)*. This section presents the main argument, that the impartial righteousness of God provides righteousness for Jews and Gentiles alike, by faith. It contains five major sections.

2. *Amplification (5:1–8:39)*. Here Paul amplifies his already-proven case, dealing with logical implications of the main idea. It consists of ten sections, with a formal introduction and conclusion.

3. *Amplification in the Style of Comparison (9:1–11:36)*. Paul proves by means of the example of unbelieving Israel that the righteousness of God will still be triumphant, that in the end the gospel will not fail. This section also consists of ten sections with an introduction and conclusion.

4. *Amplification (12:1–15:13)*. This section, like 5:1–8:39, also consists of logical implications of the main idea, though these are in the style of ethical guidelines for *living* by faith. This also consists of ten sections, with a formal introduction and conclusion.

In the next chapter, we will begin listening to the text of Paul's letter to the Romans and discussing it.

8 | Introducing Phoebe, Who Introduces Paul

Romans 1:1-17 and 15:14–16:23

Now we take our plunge into the time machine, moving back almost two millennia to the spring of 57, when Phoebe delivered Paul's letter to the Roman Christians.

From here on, each chapter of this book will deal with a part of the Romans text chosen according to the rhetorical outline discussed in chapter 7. Except for Phoebe's introduction below, all chapters will be structured in a similar way. The main idea of the passage, along with its place in the outline, will be stated, followed by a section called "Understanding the Background." Readers will then prepare themselves for the simulation. "Phoebe" or her secretary will then read the text directly from the Bible. The simulation is continued as members of each house church stay in character and discuss the questions stated or other relevant ones that come to their minds. At some point the leader will stop the simulation. Debriefing will follow, along with discussion of contemporary applications.

Understanding the Background

The material read by Phoebe and discussed in this chapter is somewhat unusual in that it is not centered around one main idea. Instead, it encloses the body of the letter and thus is just as essential. The previous seven chapters of this book have already explained most of the background needed to understand Paul's introduction and conclusion. We now know something about Paul's audience and their social, political, and theological situations. A closer look at Paul's careful introduction tells us something about his concern for being diplomatic.

Paul as a Slave

Most translations of Romans 1:1 call Paul a "servant" of Jesus Christ, but the Greek word *doulos* can be translated as either *servant* or *slave*. When we remember the ubiquitous presence of slavery in the Roman Empire, and especially among members of the Roman house churches, Paul's meaning of "slave" seems most likely (see NRSV note).

Further, if Paul is representing himself as an ambassador and using the rhetorical structure of an ambassadorial speech in his letter, he is comparing himself to slaves of the emperor who were loyal only to him and who represented him in many capacities. "During the time Paul wrote," says Jewett, "the expression 'slave of Caesar' was used for imperial ambassadors or representatives of various kinds. It was felt that such a person carried the majesty and power of the emperor as they represented him in foreign courts."[1] Some members of the households of Aristobulus and Narcissus would have been in a similar relationship with the present emperor.

An Early Christian Creed

Robert Jewett believes that the creed Paul is quoting in 1:3-5 originally belonged in an early Jewish Christian creed which stressed the Messianic line from David and the adoption of Jesus as Son of God on the basis of the resurrection.[2] This early creed may then have been edited by more liberal non-Jewish charismatic Christians, who added "according to the flesh" and "according to the Spirit," thus playing down the Jewish connection and emphasizing the Spirit. This new edition of the creed would be more attractive to people not of Jewish background.

But Paul wants unity among both Jews and Gentiles, so he uses lines from both creeds and adds two extra words "of holiness" after "according

1. Robert Jewett, *Romans,* Cokesbury Basic Bible Commentary (Nashville: Graded Press, 1987), 14.
2. Jewett, *Romans,* 15.

to the Spirit." Since holiness is a Jewish term that relates to living by God's laws, Paul seems to be trying to appeal to both conservatives and liberals right at the opening of his speech.

Who Is a Barbarian (1:14)?

In the Greco-Roman world, a barbarian was someone who could not speak Latin or Greek. This may have included some Jews and certainly most of the Spaniards. "Wise" and "foolish" probably relate to educational level, where the "foolish" would have been working-class people and slaves, without the benefit of higher education.

Paul's Collection

At the time of the apostolic conference in Jerusalem (Acts 15), Paul had promised that he would collect money for the poor in the Jerusalem church (Gal. 2:10).[3] This he has done, collecting it, according to 15:26, from the churches in Philippi and Thessalonica (in the province of Macedonia) and Corinth (in Achaia). Paul is not only concerned about the poverty of the Jerusalem Christians. Theologically, he looks at the collection as another way to unite Jews and Gentiles into one church. He reasons that since the Gentiles received the gospel through the Jews, they are in debt to the Jews and ought to seek to repay them by sharing material resources (15:27). Using a gift to convey appreciation is common.

But there are even deeper nuances involved in the Greco-Roman world. Jewett puts it like this:

> Gifts were a means of communication in that when they were received graciously, the person who was in debt was acknowledged as the equal of the person who had originally given the resource. To receive a gift, therefore, meant to acknowledge that someone else was your equal. To

3. On this further, see Acts 11:29-30; 20:1-5; 24:17; 1 Cor. 16:1-4; 2 Cor. 8–9.

give a gift was to acknowledge that you are subordinate to someone else.[4]

Knowing this background, think of the churchwide implications of the Gentiles giving a gift to the Jews, and of the Jews receiving it.

Introducing Phoebe

Who should play the role of Phoebe? The group leader or a female with a good speaking voice can be chosen from the class. If Phoebe's secretary reads, that can be a woman or a man. The reader will have to play two roles: Phoebe (or her secretary) plus a character in a Roman house church.

A person of Phoebe's importance must be carefully introduced. The most logical person to introduce her may be either Prisca or Aquila. They probably knew her while they lived in Corinth, since Cenchreae is a port city just next to Corinth. When everyone is ready to begin the simulation, Phoebe can be introduced as follows:

*   *   *

"It is my great pleasure to introduce to you Phoebe of Cenchreae. She has traveled a long way, bearing a special letter to all the Christians in Rome from our brother Paul of Tarsus.

"Phoebe comes to us with important credentials. First of all, she is our sister in Christ. Aquila (Prisca) and I met Phoebe while we were exiles in Corinth. She would come there on business and to consult with Paul or with us about her church in Cenchreae. She is your sister as well.

"Phoebe is also a deacon in the church that meets in her house. In that capacity, she oversees the community, presides over agape meals and worship, and works tirelessly to meet the spiritual and physical needs of the saints.

"Phoebe is a businesswoman, and a good one! She runs a shipping

---

4. Jewett, *Romans,* 141.

firm by the docks. This has enabled her to become a patron of many traveling missionaries of the gospel. She has supported Paul on several of his
journeys and is underwriting much of his mission to Spain. We are grateful for women like Phoebe who use their money and political influence for
the sake of the gospel.

"Last of all, Phoebe is here because she so well understands the gospel and the mind of Paul. She will be reading and interpreting Paul's letter
to us. Phoebe has told me that Paul poured his heart and soul into this letter and has entrusted the interpretation of it to her. She is excited about its
message and is eager to share it with us.

"Let us welcome Phoebe."

Phoebe Responds

"Greetings to the churches of Rome! (or the church of Prisca and Aquila or
whatever group she is greeting). I also bring you greetings from the believers in Cenchreae. They commended me to your care and pray often for
their brothers and sisters in Rome.

"I am honored to be entrusted with Paul's message to you. He longs
to be with you and indeed is with you now in spirit, as he makes the ardu-
ous journey to Jerusalem.

"Today I will read only Paul's opening and closing remarks in his letter, and his greetings to all of you who share our living hope in the gospel
of Jesus Christ."

*   *   *

Phoebe will read directly from the Bible, using the following suggestions,
or reading a paraphrase such as *The Message* by Eugene Peterson for ease
of listening. However, readers and participants must have their own
Bibles, preferably the NRSV, to use for discussion after the oral reading.
While Phoebe reads aloud, everyone should listen without following
along in the text. No house-church member would have had a copy of
Paul's letter.

Phoebe or Her Secretary Reads Romans 1:1-17 and 15:14–16:23

Introduction (1:1-7)

This letter is from "Paul, a slave of Jesus Christ, called to be an apostle, set apart for the gospel of God. . . ."

Narration — The Announcement of Paul's Mission (1:8-15)

"First, I thank my God through Jesus Christ for all of you. . . ."

Conclusion of Argument (15:14-33)

"I myself feel confident about you, brothers and sisters. . . ."

Greetings to Cell Groups and Individuals (16:1-16, 21-23)

"I commend to you our sister Phoebe, a deacon of the church at Cenchreae. . . ." While Phoebe reads the names, she can move around the room shaking hands with each member of each house church, repeating their Roman names from their name tags.

Final Benediction (16:25-27)

"Now to God who is able to strengthen you. . . ."

Questions to Discuss in Your House Church

Each person should now freely refer to her or his Bible. Use the following questions to stimulate discussion in your group. A leader should be designated by the group to begin the conversation, but persons should feel free to raise issues important to them.

1. If you are a slave or a freedperson, how does Paul's term "slave" make you feel? Does it give any new meaning to your role as a slave? What might it say about the rewards and demands of the gospel of Christ? What nuances can those slaves in the households of Aristobulus or Narcissus add to the discussion?

2. How do you feel about Paul's use and adaptation of the creed in 1:3-5? Do you think he comes across as favoring Jews or Gentiles? conservatives or liberals? Do you think he's trying too hard to appeal to everyone? What phrases in the creed do you relate to best? What phrases bother you?

3. In the ancient world rulers were often thought of as divine or as a son of deity. What might be the significance of Jesus being declared Son of God "with power"? What kind of power might Paul have in mind?

4. In 1:6-7, why is the greeting said in three phrases: "called to belong to Jesus Christ," "God's beloved in Rome," and "called to be saints"? Which phrase best describes you as Jew or Gentile?

5. Romans 1:5 and 16:26 both include the phrase "to bring about the obedience of faith among all the Gentiles." In light of the heterogeneity among the Roman house churches, what does this mean? What is "the obedience of faith"? Is it another way to blend together the spiritual and ethical aspects of the gospel, and thus to speak to both conservatives and liberals? Look for a more complete answer as we listen to the entire document of Romans.

6. In 1:8-15, what do you think of Paul's attitude? Do you like his compliments to you Christians in Rome? Or does it sound manipulative? Is Paul arrogant or humble? What do you think of his use of the word *barbarian* (1:14)? Do you consider yourself wise or foolish?

7. You have already learned about Paul's plans to bring the gospel to Spain (Rom. 15:20-24). Now you have a chance to discuss it. How do you feel about it? Is it too ambitious? Are you afraid Paul will demand too much support from you or your house church? Do you share his enthusiasm? Are the barbarian Spaniards worth it?

8. What opinions do you as a Jew or Gentile have on Paul taking a collection of money to the saints in Jerusalem? Do you think the Jerusa-

lem Jews will want to feel equal with the Gentile Christians? Do *you* want to think of both Jews and Gentiles as being equal in Christ? What might keep you from thinking that? Will you honor Paul's request to pray for him on his mission? Or do you think it's unnecessary and too risky?

9. In Romans 16, how do you feel about being mentioned by name (if you are)? Does it make you feel warmed — or suspicious? If you are a Gentile, how do you feel about Paul referring to all those Jewish refugees? Do you think he's too pro-Jewish? Would you consider accepting any of these Jews back into your house church?

Debriefing and Applying

This will be an important part of our study. After you have envisioned yourself as a first-century Christian in a house church, now is the time to come *back to the present.*

1. Think and talk about how you felt acting out a role. Do you think it worked? Was it helpful in understanding the text? If so, how? What new information have you learned, and what new insights struck you?

2. Move on to the task of interpreting and applying the text to our lives today. Now that you are out of your role, what questions would you like to ask that you couldn't ask in the first-century context?

3. If an important aspect of the gospel involves having different types of people getting along together in unity, what does this say about our contemporary situations? Should we make every effort to have unity between liberals and conservatives? between blacks, whites, and other minorities? between those who have little or much education? If we can't get along with people not like us, does that mean we are not living out the power of the gospel?

4. Do Paul's efforts at creating unity among different ethnicities and classes of people say anything about Christian attitudes toward people currently immigrating to the United States — with or without legal papers?

9 | A Gift for Everybody

Romans 1–3

Some years ago I taught first-grade children to read. Sometimes I read to them, and by the end of the year they themselves were reading stories and paragraphs. I kept asking them, "What is the *main idea* of this story (or paragraph)?" Though all of us have learned how to read, we may not be as good at figuring out the main idea of a particular piece of writing. We can get bogged down in details that support the main idea. But unless we understand the main idea, we don't really understand the writing.

This is a particular problem in Bible study. We are used to looking at a short block of text — a verse or two or a short parable — and searching for meaning from it. Such study is important, but we can much better understand the small blocks of text if we comprehend the author's overall intention and the main argument of the entire document.

In this chapter we will do two things. First, we will look at Paul's main idea or thesis, clearly stated in 1:16-17: The gospel has the power to provide righteousness for Jews and Gentiles alike — through God's grace and our faithful response.

The stated main idea of the letter — the thesis — is followed by Paul's first proof of that main idea. Here we find Paul's primary argument which proves that God makes both Jew and Gentile righteous. According to the rhetorical structure of this speech, that main argument, called the confirmation, lasts from 1:18 to the end of chapter 3 (with an explanatory example in chapter 4 which we will discuss in the next session).

Here Paul shows, painfully and depressingly, how *everyone* is alike because *everyone* has sinned. As you hear this entire section being read (while you are in your role of a Jew or Gentile in a Roman house church), listen for the more general parts of it, lists of sins that are universal. Then notice descriptions that may be more specifically related to Jewish or Gentile Christians. Which fit your house church — or you personally? Do you find it hard to listen? Do you think Paul comes down harder on one group than another: Gentiles or Jews, conservatives or liberals? Why does Paul pound away at all these monstrous sins?

Look for the answer at the end of chapter 3. Paul makes the case for human evil as grim as he can so that he can show how God impartially extends grace and salvation to everyone, regardless of their works. Boasting in one's self-righteousness is excluded.

Outline of the Main Argument

- Human idolatry and divine wrath are revealed (1:18-32).
- God sends righteous judgment on Jews and Gentiles (2:1-29).
- Jews are involved in universal sin (3:1-20).
- All are made righteous by faith alone (3:21-31).
- Abraham is the example of faith (4:1-25).

Understanding the Background

What Does Righteousness Mean?

The Greek word *dikaioō* (di-kai-O-ō) can be translated either "to make righteous" or "to declare and treat as righteous"; in short form, we say "to justify." The problem is that in English, *righteousness* has a connotation different from *justification*. *Righteous* conveys to us a sense of goodness, wholeness, integrity, and upright living, while we tend to think of *justified* as a legal term meaning we are considered good even though we have done wrong. But when this happens, "justification by faith alone" — a Lutheran emphasis which means "freedom from condemnation" — is separated from the "righteousness of God."

To minimize this translation problem, Robert Jewett suggests using an old English word, "rightwising." This carries more the idea of setting things right and achieving "a transformation in which humans come to reflect the righteousness of God."[1]

Righteousness and Ecology

People of Paul's day would view life much more collectively than individualistically. For those with Jewish connections, the phrase "the righteousness of God is revealed" (1:17) would bring to mind the Jewish expectation that at the end of time God would be revealed, triumph over enemies, and bring the kingdom of God to earth. Since the curse of Genesis 3 is also a curse on the earth, the revealing of God's righteousness also means an ecological restoration.

Who Are the "Jews"?

We assume that the references to Jews mean Jewish Christians, since Paul was writing only to the Christian house churches. The Jewish community as a whole was faithfully observing the traditional Jewish Law and did not find it a burden. On the other hand, there must have been some Jewish Christians violating the principle of God's impartial grace by fostering rivalry among competing house churches and not accepting those who did not keep that Law.

Romans 2:17-22 contains a list of upright behaviors that Jewish people would consider important to perform. But Paul shows how these actions can be and have been perverted. Regarding the accusation of robbing temples, Paul may be referring to the fact that some Jews would actually steal gifts from pagan temples, since the owners — the so-called gods — didn't exist anyway![2]

---

1. Jewett, *Romans*, 24.

2. Dunn, *Romans 1–8*, Word Biblical Commentary, vol. 38A (Waco, Tex.: Word Books, 1988), 114-115.

Salvation by Faith Alone

The ringing climax of this confirmation is 3:21-31, where Paul, after showing that *everyone* has sinned, now shows how *everyone* can be rightwised — through Jesus Christ. Paul uses three different phrases to explain how salvation through Christ works. Jewett sees this technique as a way to appeal to different groups of people in Rome.[3] The first is in 3:24, "through the redemption that is in Christ Jesus." Redemption refers to buying slaves and releasing them from captivity, a term appropriate for all the slaves who were members of house-church groups in Rome.

The second in 3:25a speaks of expiation, "a sacrifice of atonement by [Christ's] blood." Christians with a Jewish background would have best understood this phrase because it refers to the sprinkling of blood on the altar in the Jerusalem temple on the Day of Atonement (Lev. 16:12-15). Jewish Christians regarded the blood of animals as replaced by Jesus' blood, through which they could now be forgiven.

The third phrase, in 3:25b, says that "in [God's] divine forbearance [God] had passed over the sins previously committed." For Christians with less contact with Judaism, such unconditional forgiveness would have been most meaningful. But "pass over" can also mean "leave unpunished."[4] God's overlooking Gentile sins may have been hard for some Jews to swallow, since they had so often been victims of Gentile oppression and brutality throughout their history.

Now listen while Phoebe reads, beginning with the thesis statement. (Please note that numerous supporting details are left out so the main idea can more easily be seen. Use the full biblical text for discussion and study questions.)

---

3. Jewett, *Romans*, 52.

4. John E. Toews, *Romans*, Believers Bible Commentary (Scottdale, Pa.; Waterloo, Ont.: Herald Press, 2004).

Phoebe or Her Secretary Reads Romans 1–3

The Thesis Statement (1:16-17)

"For I am not ashamed of the gospel; it is the power of God for salvation to everyone who has faith, to the Jew first and also to the Greek. For in it the righteousness of God is revealed through faith for faith; as it is written, 'the one who is righteous will live by faith.'"

Human Idolatry and Divine Wrath Are Revealed (1:18-32)

1:18-23 "For the wrath of God is revealed. . . ."[5]
    1:28-32 "And since they did not see fit to acknowledge God. . . ."

God Sends Righteous Judgment on Jews and Gentiles (2:1-29)

2:1-2 "Therefore you have no excuse. . . ." (Skip 2:3-8.)
    2:9-11 "There will be anguish and distress for everyone who does evil. . . ."
    2:12-14 "All who have sinned apart from the law will also perish apart from the law. . . ."
    2:17, 21-29 "But if you call yourself a Jew. . . ."

---

5. Our contemporary obsession with the issue of homosexuality should not overshadow Paul's main idea. However, the following observations should be noted: (1) Homosexual practice is a result of idolatry, not a cause of it. (2) Paul never discusses homosexual orientation, since the term itself did not exist, and ancient Greco-Romans assumed people were bisexual. Homosexual practice was common and often highly regarded. (3) Jews associated homosexual relations with idolatry, and Paul is writing out of a Jewish understanding. (4) Slaves of both sexes had no rights to their own bodies and were often raped by their owners or others socially superior to them. Both male and female slaves would have found Paul's condemnation of lustful, out-of-control sexual behavior liberating. On this last point, see Robert Jewett, "The Social Context and Implications of Homoerotic References in Romans," in *Homosexuality, Science, and the "Plain Sense" of Scripture,* ed. David L. Balch (Grand Rapids: Eerdmans, 2000), 239, who refers to the normalcy, in that male-dominated society, of intercourse between male masters and male slaves.

Jews Are Involved in Universal Sin (3:1-20)

3:1-4a "Then what advantage has the Jew? . . ."

 3:5-6 "But if our injustice serves to show the justice of God, what shall we say? . . ."

 3:9-11, 20 "What then? Are Jews any better off? . . ."

All Are Made Righteous by Faith Alone (3:21-31)

3:21-25 "But now, apart from the law, the righteousness of God has been disclosed. . . ."

 3:27-30a "Then what becomes of boasting? . . ."

Questions to Discuss in Your House Church

If you are part of a simulation, discuss these questions in your house church. If you have developed your own character(s) while reading this book, these questions will help you focus on Paul's main argument.

Questions about the Thesis Statement

1. How do you as Jews or Gentiles feel about being included together in the thesis statement of 1:16-17? Is it discriminatory that Paul says "Jew first"? Do Jews feel Gentiles should not be included?
2. Explain the meaning of this phrase: "In [the gospel] the righteousness of God is revealed." Do you see it revealed in yourself, in your house church, or in Rome? How?
3. As Jews or Gentiles, do you see the gospel being this kind of power? Do you consider yourself a part of it? As a Gentile, do you feel the Christian Jews you know are including you in on this vision of the gospel?

Questions about the First Argument (1:18–3:31)

If you are a Gentile . . .

1. How do you feel about Paul's strong words? Is he being realistic about the state of the human race? Do you resent any of it? Does Paul step on your toes? Is Paul evenhanded when including both Jews and Gentiles in sin?

2. Given what you know about the religions in Rome — the old pantheon of gods, emperor worship, mysteries — what evidence do you see of people worshiping the creature instead of the Creator? Is Paul right?

3. What do you think about Paul's numerous Scripture quotations? Do you understand them? Christian faith has its roots in the Hebrew Scriptures and Jewish history and tradition. Does that bother you? Are you annoyed that Jesus was a Jew and that "the Jews were entrusted with the oracles of God" (3:2)? How does that fit with Paul's main thesis?

4. As a Gentile with conservative leanings, are you judgmental toward more-liberal Christians in any of the house churches? How did you feel about 2:1-11? Is Paul too hard on you for your complaints about more liberal Christians?

5. The climax of Paul's argument in the first three chapters is 3:21-26. Which of the three explanations of salvation makes most sense to you as a Gentile? If you are a slave, which appeals most to you?

6. Does this first confirmation of Paul's thesis help you better understand Jewish Christians or those more conservative than you are? Why or why not? Does it change your opinion about any other house church or make you feel less antagonistic toward members there?

If you are Jewish . . .

If you are a man or a woman with some education, you likely have a good bit of knowledge of Torah (the Old Testament). If possible, look up the references Paul makes to Scriptures in a study Bible before you participate in the discussion.[6] More will be expected of you.

1. Is Paul too hard on Jewish Christians? Are you as sinful as he seems to imply? How do you feel about the importance of circumcision?
2. Do you think Paul uses enough respect when talking about your Jewish heritage? Do you agree with the conclusion of Paul's argument in 3:21-31 that God's righteousness is shown *apart* from the Law to all those who believe? Or do you think Paul is talking out of two sides of his mouth, since he says in 3:31 that "we uphold the Law"? What attitude do you take toward the Law in your own life and practice?
3. Read #4 under "If you are a Gentile," and apply it to yourself as a Jew.
4. If you are a Jewish refugee, do you think what you have heard from Paul will make it easier for you to reenter your former house church?

If you are a Jewish woman . . .

What do you think of all this discussion about circumcision and uncircumcision? In this respect, does the gospel of Christ seem more accepting and gender-blind than Judaism, in which only males received the mark of the covenant through circumcision?

For everyone . . .

What is Jesus' role in this discussion of what the gospel is? (See 3:23-25.) Put in your own words what Jesus' salvation means to you in your situation as Jew or Gentile, poor or not-so-poor, educated or uneducated, slave or free.

6. You can use a study Bible such as *The New Oxford Annotated Bible: New Revised Standard Version* (New York: Oxford University Press, 1991).

Debriefing and Applying

Now move back into the twenty-first century. What did you learn from the simulation? Did you find it easy or difficult to stay in character? Why? What questions do you now want to ask that you couldn't ask then?

1. Put in your own words Paul's main theme in his letter to the Romans. If you grasp that now, it will help you better comprehend the rest of the letter.
2. Do you think human nature is still as evil as Paul seemed to think it was then? If you think human sin should not be stressed so much, how can God's impartial grace be emphasized? Does grace mean anything without recognition of sin and weakness and inadequacy?
3. To what persons or groups of people in your school, church, or society do you feel morally superior? How would Paul respond?
4. Self-esteem is an important issue in our present culture. Everyone wants to feel good about themselves. When someone isn't functioning well, we often blame their problems on low self-esteem. Would Paul's argument in Romans 1:16–4:25 help or hurt a person's self-esteem? If you feel Paul is out of sync with contemporary psychology, with which way of looking at human nature do you feel more comfortable? Which attitude do you believe is right? Does it make a difference if you are a man or a woman?
5. How might Paul's approach parallel Alcoholics Anonymous (or other Anonymous groups) in their practice of admitting that they are still alcoholics always in need of a Higher Power?

10 | An Example from the Scriptures

Romans 4

A few years ago I was talking with a friend who considered herself to be an evangelical Christian committed to the Bible. Some of us were struggling to understand what the Bible says about homosexual practice and what attitude we should take toward gay and lesbian people. I asked this friend what she thought about the prohibition of male homosexual practice in Leviticus 18:22. Why should we obey that verse if we don't pay attention to similar rules against women having sexual intercourse while menstruating (Lev. 18:19), eating meat and milk products together (Exod. 23:19), or wearing fabric composed of both linen and wool (Deut. 22:11)?

I thought she would have a well-researched response. Instead she said, "Actually, I don't pay that much attention to the Old Testament. I think it's mainly the New Testament that's important for Christians."

I was flabbergasted that someone who considered herself a biblical Christian would give such a reply. However, since then I have had to admit that many Christians — including those who call themselves "Bible-believing" — don't pay much attention to the Old Testament, other than occasionally telling a story to children in Sunday school.

However, for the earliest Christians, it was not so. They did not have a New Testament. Their Bible was primarily what we now call the Old Testament, and they — at least those who were Jews or had Jewish connections — used it constantly for study, memorization, worship, and singing. Actually, they did not have a strict canon of thirty-nine books, as we do today. That came later. But they read all the books we use today, as well as being familiar with Jewish literature written during what we now call the intertestamental period, from about 350 B.C. to the first century A.D. The

Old Testament canon was not closed until some years after the temple in Jerusalem had fallen in A.D. 70.

Around the third century B.C., the Hebrew Bible was translated into Greek, called the Septuagint (sep-TOO-a-gint; from seventy, the approximate number of its translators, according to legend).[1] Greek-speaking Jews were more familiar with the Septuagint than the Hebrew Bible, since they primarily spoke Greek. When Paul quotes from the Old Testament, he uses the Septuagint.

As a Jew thoroughly trained in his traditions, the apostle Paul had studied the Scriptures intensely. After he met Jesus on the road to Damascus, he had to rethink his entire worldview and theology. But he did not do it by ignoring the Scriptures and depending only on his own insights and the illumination of the Holy Spirit. Rather, he was going through a major process of reinterpreting the Old Testament, showing how the Law, the wisdom writings, and the Prophets pointed toward Jesus as the promised Messiah and deliverer of the Jews. This same Jesus was fulfilling prophecies that through the Jews the Gentiles would find salvation.

All of Paul's letters are full of references to the Old Testament, but Romans is especially saturated. According to one scholar, there are ninety-three quotations from the Old Testament in all the Pauline letters, *fifty-three of which occur in Romans.*[2] Why so many quotations in Romans? Because the letter has to do with God's saving righteousness for both Jews and Gentiles.[3]

On one hand, Paul is a Jew through and through and firmly believes in one God, Yahweh, who has called the people of Israel to Yahweh's salvation. At the same time, Paul is also convinced that Jesus has come for Gentiles as well, and that he, Paul, is commissioned to tell them. Combine Paul's apostolic commission with his concern for the frictions in the Ro-

---

1. For the legend, see the Letter of Aristeas, in James H. Charlesworth, ed., *The Old Testament Pseudepigrapha*, vol. 2 (New York: Doubleday, 1985), 7-34. Aristeas says there were seventy-two translators, six from each tribe; Josephus in *Antiquities* 12.2.7 also says six from each tribe alongside the number 70! (cf. Exod. 24:1; Num. 11:16; Luke 10:1).

2. E. Earle Ellis, *Paul's Use of the Old Testament* (Edinburgh: Oliver and Boyd, 1957), 150-52. This includes six from Ephesians and the Pastorals, which Ellis treats as Pauline.

3. Richard B. Hays, *Echoes of Scripture in the Letters of Paul* (New Haven: Yale University Press, 1989), 34.

man house churches between Jews and Gentiles, liberals and conservatives — and you have a letter insisting that the gospel is the *fulfillment*, not the negation, of God's word to Israel.

One of the questions we can ask during this study of Romans is about Paul's method of interpreting the Scriptures. How does he do it? As persons simulating characters in the Roman churches, do we agree with his method of using Scripture? As modern Christians, how do Paul's methods compare with how we interpret the Old Testament today?

Romans 4 is a wonderful example of how Paul uses the Scriptures. He makes Abraham a test case for his thesis and confirmation of Romans 1–3. Does the story of Abraham prove that both Gentiles and Jews can be rightwised by their faith alone, or does it emphasize Israel's supremacy? Paul makes a case for Abraham being the father of *both* Gentiles and Jews (4:16-17). Because of that, non-Jewish Christians today also claim Abraham as one of our forefathers in the faith.

But it was not always so obvious. Indeed, one of the big theological battles Paul had to fight was with Jewish Christians who believed God wanted the Gentiles to keep the same religious laws as Jews in order to be saved. This was no abstract argument. It had to do with nitty-gritty things like the foods one ate, the holidays one celebrated, or whether or not adult Gentile men would have to undergo the painful operation of circumcision. Later in the letter Paul does carefully deal with these concrete issues.

Understanding the Background

Before you listen to Romans 4 or read it, a few morsels of background material will enrich this text.

Old Testament Texts

The primary text Paul uses is Genesis 15:6, which he quotes almost verbatim in 4:3. "And [Abraham] believed the LORD; and the LORD reckoned it to him as righteousness." This refers to God's promise to the aging, childless Abraham that he would have a biological son and through him have descendants as numerous as the stars. Anyone not familiar with the story of Abraham and Sarah should read Genesis 12:1–25:10, or at least, for our purposes, chapters 12–17 and 21:1-7. Those with Jewish connections in the Roman house churches were familiar with the story of Abraham and Sarah, the original Hebrew foreparents.

Romans 4:9-11 speaks of Abraham's circumcision, referring to Genesis 17:23-27, when he was circumcised at the age of 99, at least fourteen years *after* the setting of Genesis 15:6, where he believes God's promise and it is reckoned to him for righteousness.

The secondary text is a psalm of David, Psalm 32:1-2, where Paul emphasizes that the blessed, happy, and rightwised people are not those who never do anything wrong, but those who are forgiven.

Translation Difficulties

Romans 4:1 (NRSV) reads, "What then are we to say was gained by Abraham, our ancestor according to the flesh?" However, Pauline scholar Richard Hays insists that such a translation runs recklessly over the Greek text. It should say, "What then shall we say? Have we found Abraham to be our forefather according to the flesh?"[4]

Hays says Paul's answer to these questions is emphatically NO. Paul uses the rest of the chapter to make that case because he maintains that Judaism itself, rightly understood, also believes that trusting God is the issue, and not biological relationship.

An Example of Intertestamental Jewish Thought

However, the Judaism of Paul's time was not so clear on the above issue. James Dunn sees Paul attacking head-on the current, widely accepted Jewish way of thinking about Abraham — which was as a model for the de-

---

4. Hays, *Echoes of Scripture,* 54.

vout, law-abiding Jew.[5] It was even being said that Abraham observed the Law even though it was not yet written![6]

One of the intertestamental writings which Paul certainly would have known is Ecclesiasticus, or Ben Sirach, in the Apocrypha of the Old Testament (found in some Bibles). This collection of poetry was written about 190 B.C. and translated into Greek about 130 B.C.[7] This is what Ben Sirach writes about Abraham in 44:19-21:

> Abraham was the great father of a multitude of nations,
>   and no one has been found like him in glory.
> He kept the law of the Most High,
>   and entered into a covenant with him;
> he certified the covenant in his flesh,
>   and when he was tested he proved faithful.
> Therefore the Lord assured him with an oath
>   that the nations would be blessed through his offspring
> that he would make him as numerous as the dust of the earth,
>   and exalt his posterity like the stars,
> and give them an inheritance from sea to sea
>   and from the Euphrates to the ends of the earth.

This passage emphasizes (1) that Abraham kept the law *before* he received the promise of posterity, and (2) that Abraham's posterity, the Jews, would be exalted above others. Whether or not Paul had this passage in mind when he wrote Romans 4, he uses the Genesis material to draw conclusions *opposite* to Ben Sirach.

---

5. Dunn, *Romans 1–8*, 226.

6. One of several places where this can be found is in Jubilees 16:28. Jubilees, a Jewish document from the second century B.C., retells the stories of Genesis with some omissions and many embellishments that go far beyond our biblical text. Jubilees can be found in Charlesworth, *The Old Testament Pseudepigrapha*, vol. 2, 45-142.

7. "Introduction to Ecclesiasticus," in *The Jerusalem Bible* (New York: Doubleday, 1966), 1034.

Creating out of Nothing

In 4:17 Paul quotes part of an early Christian confession (the midverse dash in the NRSV signals the rough transition to confessional material).[8] He quotes: "in the presence of the God in whom [Abraham] believed, who gives life to the dead and calls into existence the things that do not exist." Thus God "calls" something into existence, and God calls it out of nothing. These ideas were held by both early Christians and Hellenistic Jews. Such a philosophical interest in creation was distinctively Greek.[9]

In this way Paul links God's power in rightwising Abraham and giving him a son in old age with God's power as Creator. In 4:24-25, this power of giving life to the dead is in turn linked to Jesus' resurrection and the salvation of human beings.

Phoebe or Her Secretary Reads Romans 4:1-25

What about Abraham? (4:1-3, 6-8)

"What then shall we say? Have we found Abraham to be our forefather according to the flesh? No! For if . . ." (Hays). (See Gen. 15:6; Ps. 32:1-2).

Faith and Righteousness as Above (4:10-11)

"How then was [righteousness] reckoned to [Abraham]? . . ."

True Heirs of Abraham (4:13-14, 16-17, 19, 23-25)

"For the promise . . . [faith] will be reckoned to us who believe in him who raised Jesus our Lord from the dead, who was handed over to death for our trespasses and was raised [so we could be made righteous]."

---

8. Jewett, *Romans*, 56. Cf. Rom. 4:17 with 2 Macc, 7:28 and Wisd. of Sol. 11:24-25, both in the Apocrypha; Heb. 11:3.

9. Jewett, *Romans*, 56.

Questions to Discuss in Your House Church

1. Do you think Paul uses the example of Abraham with integrity? Or is he taking a true-blue Jewish story and twisting it to fit his own ideas about faith and the Law? What do you think of his method of interpreting the Scriptures?

2. How well do you think this example illustrates the point Paul is making in Romans 1:16–3:31?

3. How do you as a Gentile or a Jew react to Paul's teaching here? Do you have differences of opinion in your house church? If you do, are you dividing along racial lines, or more along liberal-conservative lines?

4. If you are more conservative and think Paul is misinterpreting the text about Abraham in Genesis, do you prefer Ben Sirach's line? Do you believe Jews have special brownie points with God because they are biological descendants of Abraham or keep the law? What would you like the Gentiles in your house church to do about this? Should they keep all the Jewish laws? Should they spend more time studying the Scriptures?

5. If you agree with Paul, how will you get along with your brothers and sisters in Christ who don't agree?

Debriefing and Applying

Now move back into the twenty-first century. What did you learn from the simulation? Did you stay in character? What questions do you now want to ask that you couldn't ask then?

1. How important do you think it is that Christians study and understand our Old Testament?

2. Does this chapter make you wonder why you should even try to do right and live a good life, since God forgives sins and does not seem impressed by the good works a Christian might do? In other words, does Paul make his case too strongly?

3. Do you know of some Christian churches or groups who have split over this issue of salvation through good works versus salvation through faith? What about your church group or home congregation?

11 | The Old Adam and the New Christ

Romans 5–6

On Easter Sunday 1992, two Mennonite comedians, Ted and Lee, performed one of their routines at Community Mennonite Church in Harrisonburg, Virginia. Reenacting the resurrection story, they played the roles of less-than-bright Peter and Andrew hiding fearfully in an upper room after the crucifixion of Jesus. Jesus apparently enters, and in shock and awe they reach out and touch him. Then he disappears.

"That was *Jesus!*" says Peter, the enthusiastic know-it-all.

"I know. But — what does it MEAN?" puzzles Andrew.

"It means — well, that he's alive!"

"I know. But . . . but . . . what does that MEAN?"

"It means he's no longer dead!"

"I know that. But . . . but . . . what does that MEAN?"

"It means he's the Messiah!"

"I know. But . . . but . . . what does that MEAN?"

"It means he's the promised one."

"I know. But . . . but . . . what does that MEAN?"

No doubt the skit was — among other things — a spoof on theology classes where professors keep prodding students to think through the implications of profound theological truths. If the apostle Paul had heard this skit, he no doubt would have stood up and preached a long sermon on exactly what Jesus' resurrection MEANS! Indeed, Paul's entire letter to the Romans can be seen as a single thesis statement about what the gospel is (1:16-17), followed by four proofs telling us exactly what he thinks it means. We have just examined the first proof in 1:18–4:25. Jews and non-Jews are equal because all have sinned, and God's grace is inclusive for both groups equally.

We now begin looking at the second proof, dealing with the implications of the first proof. So everyone has sinned and the only way to be rightwised is through the grace of God made known in Jesus. What does that mean? Romans 5–8 gives us the first explanation. For one thing, says Paul in chapter 5, if we have this free gift of being made righteous, it works itself outward to create peace and reconciliation. Sin and death came to every human being because of one person, Adam. Now life and peace come to everyone through one person, Jesus Christ. The more sin increases, the more grace abounds.

We can just hear the Roman Christians asking, "But what does that MEAN? Does it mean we should sin all the more so God's grace can abound all the more?" This launches Paul into chapter 6, where he says, Absolutely not! Those who belong to the New Order don't behave like they are still part of the Old Order. Holiness is the logical outcome of living under grace.

When we read these chapters from the viewpoint of present-day Protestant American individualism, we tend to think that Paul is speaking, if not of legal justification, at least of devotional piety, or at most, of private morality. We may think of boring abstractions, of dogmas learned in church about the way one is saved and justified. But these often have little connection with our everyday lives.

However, Paul was thinking concretely and specifically about those squabbling Christian communities in Rome. Since they are being made righteous, how will that work itself out in the way they actually get along with each other — both within their cell groups and as cell groups relating to each other? How do slaves get along with freedpersons? How do people with labor-intensive, low-paying jobs get along with those who have cushy jobs that pay better? How do those who still think the Jewish law is important tolerate those who flout the law? If you are playing the role of one character in a house church, you will hear these chapters in a different way than ever before.

Because of the length and significance of Paul's second proof, Romans 5–8 will be divided into three lessons. This one will deal with chapters 5–6. Altogether, there are ten sections for the second proof. Only the first four sections are included below, along with their subsections.

- Introduction to the Argument (5:1-11)
    1. Peace in the midst of affliction (5:1-2)
    2. Afflictions and sufferings (5:3-5)
    3. Reconciliation with God (5:6-10)
    4. Summary statement (5:11)
- The Realms of Adam and Christ (5:12-21)
    1. Introduction (5:12)
    2. Sin in the garden of Eden (5:13-14)
    3. Adam and Christ are compared (5:15-21)
- Sin and Baptism (6:1-14)
- Sin, Lordship, and Sanctification (6:15-23)[1]

Understanding the Background

The Grammar of Peace

In most versions of the New Testament, Romans 5:1 reads, "Since we are justified by faith, *we have* peace with God. . . ." But many of the most ancient Greek manuscripts do not make this a simple statement. Instead, the verb "have" is subjunctive and should be translated "let us have."

This changes the emphasis a great deal. Instead of a more Protestant understanding that everything is now all worked out and we already have some abstract, pie-in-the-sky peace, we now have a more Anabaptist call to *peace-making*. If the message of the first proof is true, then we are called to *make* peace and work out reconciliation with God and with each other.

Suffering

What might Paul mean by suffering? At this time, the Roman Christians are not undergoing a widespread persecution by the government. Yet life for slaves and poor freed-persons, as well as poor freepersons, always involves

1. Outlines are from Jewett, *Romans,* 60, 69.

physical suffering. They are in overcrowded tenements, with a limited choice of foods, which often leads to poor health, inadequate medical care, a water supply carried through lead pipes (now known to be toxic), and hard work often producing little income. As added pressure, the Roman Christians are now expected to welcome back the Jewish Christian refugees and help them and their families get settled in already overcrowded conditions.

As if that isn't enough, friction has developed. Returning refugees have learned some different theology while away and want to teach it to the Christians who never left Rome. New Gentile leaders have sprung up in the cell groups and are not necessarily interested in changing their ways. They have developed some of their own theology in the absence of Jewish leaders, and they like things the way they are. In spite of such problems, Paul seems to think that such suffering is actually good for Christians — even worth boasting about.

The "Good Person" of 5:7

Read the section under "Benefactors" in chapter 15 of this book. The system of patronage throughout the Roman Empire encouraged wealthy people to contribute money, prestige, or other gifts for the public good. On Roman inscriptions, these benefactors were often called "noble and good" or "righteous and good."[2] Paul is allowing that someone might be willing to die for such a wonderful benefactor. But he contrasts such a noble action with God's greater love, shown in that Jesus died for us even though we are not great benefactors but just plain sinners.

Paul's Exuberance Affects His Sentence Structure

Notice that 5:12 is not a complete sentence. Paul begins a statement contrasting sin and righteousness, and then cuts it off after only the negative

2. Bruce W. Winter, "The Public Honouring of Christian Benefactors: Romans 13:3-4 and 1 Peter 2:14-15," *Journal for the Study of the New Testament* 34 (1988): 87-90.

half of the sentence. He is diverted into explaining *how* sin and death came through one man, and he doesn't complete his thought until verse 18! If Phoebe or her secretary reads that section carefully, no doubt listeners who know Paul are smiling at his enthusiastic disregard for sentence structure.[3]

Sin Comes through Adam and Eve

In the previous chapter of this book, we noticed Paul developing theological ideas in direct opposition to some Jewish doctrines of his day. But now, when speaking of Adam as responsible for sin having come into the world (5:12-19), Paul depends on current Jewish thought. He refers to the Fall in Genesis 3, a text Jews at that time were using to wrestle with the problems of evil and death.[4] (The Old Testament Scriptures do not otherwise refer to Adam and Eve as the origin of sin.) But Paul is unlike Ben Sirach (25:24), who says that "from a woman [Eve] sin had its beginning, and because of her we all die." Instead, Paul places the responsibility on Adam.

Baptism as Initiation

In chapter 5 of this book, reread the section on "Personal Religion — The Mysteries." Members of Roman house churches with some experience in a mystery religion may be able to grasp the importance and power of baptism as a symbol for the Christian's initiation into Christ's resurrection. At the same time, Jewish believers and Gentiles who were "God-fearers" are familiar with baptism as a Jewish rite practiced by John the Baptist, now widely used as an initiatory ritual for Christians. Sometime in the first century, baptism was also introduced for proselytes (converts) to Judaism.[5] To strengthen the imagery, Jews could understand being buried under water

---

3. Dunn, *Romans 1–8*, 290.

4. Dunn, *Romans 1–8*, 289.

5. Lars Hartmann, "Baptism," *The Anchor Bible Dictionary*, ed. D. N. Freedman (New York: Doubleday, 1992), 1:583.

in baptism as a symbol of death, since Jews buried their dead in underground catacombs. (Non-Jews were generally cremated.)

Preparing for Simulation

Think through what kinds of suffering you are presently undergoing, if any. How well do you understand Adam and Eve and the Fall? Read Genesis 3 if you need to refresh your memory.

Phoebe or Her Secretary Reads Romans 5–6

Consequences of Being Made Righteous (5:1-5)

"Therefore, since we are made righteous by faith, *let us have peace with God* through our Lord Jesus Christ. Through him we have obtained access to this grace in which we stand, and we rejoice in our hope of sharing the glory of God. More than that, we also rejoice in our sufferings. . . ."

Reconciled to God (5:6-11)

"Imagine! While we were still weak and ungodly, Christ died for us! . . . Now we're God's friends instead of his enemies."

Adam and Christ (5:12-21)

"Therefore, just as sin came into the world through one man, [Adam,] and death through sin. . . . Just as sin was responsible for death, so grace is responsible for rightwising leading to eternal life through Jesus Christ our Lord."

United with Christ in Baptism (6:1-11)

"What shall we say then? Shall we continue in sin so that grace may increase? Absolutely not! How can we who died to sin still live in it? Don't you know that all of us who have been baptized into Christ Jesus were baptized into his death? We were buried with him by baptism into death, so that as Christ was raised from the dead by the glory of the Father, we too might walk in newness of life. . . ."

Yield Yourselves to God (6:12-13)

"Then don't let sin reign in your mortal bodies, to make you obey their passions. Instead, yield yourselves to God as those who have been brought from death to life, and the various parts of your bodies as instruments of righteousness."

Enslaved to God (6:15-23)

"What then? Are we to sin because we are not under law but under grace? Absolutely not! . . ."

Questions to Discuss in Your House Church

1. What suffering are you enduring at present? Does any of it relate to the homelessness of returning refugees or to your inconveniences because they have returned? What do you think about the task of making peace and being reconciled with God and with your Christian brothers and sisters in your own cell group and in other groups? Do you think this is necessary? With whom are you having a difficult time being reconciled — at work, at home, with your friends, in your house church, or in other house church groups?

2. In 5:12, Paul seems to make two contradictory statements: (1) that sin

is all Adam's fault, and (2) that everyone is responsible for their own sin. Where do you think sin originated? As a Gentile, do you know and accept the story of Adam and Eve? As a woman, how do you feel about Eve not being mentioned here? Is that a compliment to women, is it sexist, or is it neither? Why do you think Paul only refers to Adam?

3. In chapter 6, do you agree with Paul's logic that one should live a holy, ethical life under grace and even apart from the law? For those from pagan backgrounds and polytheistic religions, how do you feel about your religious faith having such a strong ethical, practical dimension? What might "newness of life" (6:4) mean in your specific situation in Rome?

4. What purpose do you see in baptism? Is Paul referring to a specific, physical water baptism? (Have you been thus baptized?) Or is he speaking figuratively? Is it possible that literal baptism could become part of the "law" that Paul says will not save people? Or is it absolutely necessary for salvation? How can it play a positive role?

5. Since so many of you are either slaves or freed slaves, how do you feel about Paul's imagery of slavery? Is it insulting — or easy to understand because it is so relevant to your life? Can one ever experience absolute freedom?

6. Some members of your group may be new Christians with little knowledge of Judaism or even the Scriptures. Have several of the more educated people explain in their own words to the whole group what they think are the main ideas in this section of Paul's letter.

Debriefing and Applying

After the simulation, discuss what you learned from this text. Were you able to stay in character? What questions do you want to ask now that you couldn't ask then?

1. How can the main ideas of this text be applied to contemporary life? Now that slavery is no longer legal, does Paul's imagery feel out of

date? Or do modern concepts of obsessions and addictions provide parallels? What might individuals or groups be enslaved to today? Alcohol or other substances? A consumer lifestyle? The need to succeed and get ahead of other people? What else?

2. Can Paul's message about making peace and being reconciled with God and brothers and sisters be contemporized to your lives? When there is hostility between you and someone else, how do you work it out? Is it possible to be alive in Christ and carry unresolved grudges? Does lack of peace on an interpersonal level prevent one from having peace with God?

3. Paul speaks of sanctification or holiness as the result of living by the grace of God and being a slave of righteousness. What is holiness? Is this something you want to strive for, or does it feel stuffy? What kind of holiness would be attractive to you? Has our culture misinterpreted real holiness because most people aren't interested in accepting God's free gift of eternal life and becoming holy?

12 | Keeping the Rules Is a Trap!

Romans 7

As a young man, Martin Luther joined an order of Augustinian monks, longing to follow God as perfectly as he could. With great zeal, he followed the rules of the monastery and spent hours on his knees in prayer. Yet he always felt burdened by guilt. No matter how hard he tried, the feeling of being "not okay" persisted.

Today we might scoff at the things young man Luther did to try to gain salvation, but our feelings of guilt may be just as strong in other areas. Food, for example, is essential for survival, but countless Americans are engaged in daily battle with it, always knowing they are eating too much and the wrong kind of it, and hating themselves when they gain back pounds so laboriously lost. We also hate or envy others when they *do* reach their goals or when they seem to do effortlessly what we struggle so hard to achieve. In thousands of ways, our culture sets up norms, and when we don't or can't conform, we feel inadequate.

Having such feelings of guilt and anxiety, envy and pride, many Christians instantly identify with Paul's words in Romans 7:19: "I do not do the good I want, but the evil I do not want is what I do."

But is this what Paul meant? Did Paul still feel conflicted about his behavior after he was a Christian? Or does it refer to his pre-Christian experience? And what does this have to say about our lives as Christians? If Paul only felt conflicted *before* he was converted, and we still feel that way *after* we've become Christians, does that mean we're still not saved, or not accepted by God? Perhaps Paul wasn't talking about himself. Was he referring to everyman and everywoman, and hinting that no human being can escape this treadmill?

*   *   *

These questions may be the wrong ones to ask at the start of a study on Romans 7. It is too easy to read our contemporary experiences back into a first-century document, and consequently misinterpret it. Rather, we need to stay with our friends in Rome, hearing these words as they would have first heard them, and seeing how this chapter fits into Paul's entire argument throughout his letter.

Chapter 7 is still part of the second proof of Paul's thesis of how the gospel of Christ is the power of God for the salvation of both Jews and Gentiles. In the preceding lesson on Romans 5 and 6, we noticed how sin and death are contrasted with righteousness, and how the believer who has been accepted by God is to live as a slave of righteousness rather than of sin.

Now Paul throws in a further complicating factor, something he had laid aside since his first proof in chapters 1–4: the Law. Of course. He is a good Jewish rabbi who knows the Law well, and he is speaking to those who also know the Law, both Jewish Christians and Gentile God-worshipers. The Mosaic Law was the method by which God mediated grace to Jews.

What role then does the Law play in this juxtaposition of opposites: sin and death on one side of the seesaw, and righteousness on the other? We may have gotten the idea from Romans 2 that the Mosaic Law was bad because some Jews were breaking it and because no matter how well one tried to keep the Law, that would never be a way to gain brownie points with God.

But Paul does not say the Law is bad; in 7:12 he calls it holy, and in 7:14 he calls it spiritual. Paul never tosses the Law on the sin-and-death side of the seesaw. Rather, Paul sees the Mosaic Law as the fulcrum that holds up the seesaw. The Law shows those who observe it what sin is — and it can also show us what grace and righteousness are.

But exactly *how* does the Law point up sin? Western culture has been so influenced by Martin Luther's concept of sin and guilt that we assume Paul saw the Law as impossible to keep. We *think* Paul said the Law was an ideal set of rules, and if one kept them all, one would be happy and righteous and enjoy God's love. But there were so many laws that no matter how hard one tried, some minor rule would be overlooked, and the whole house of cards would come tumbling down. Guilt would envelop the lawbreaker, who would feel hated by God. Using this logic, the Law must be evil and should be thrown out entirely.

Unfortunately, reading Paul's letters in this way — especially Romans 7 — has been disastrous. For one thing, it has encouraged many people not to worry about ethics and holiness, since God has accepted them just as they are anyway. All one needs to do is say one believes in Christ, and it doesn't matter a great deal how one lives.

Second, it has produced centuries of anti-Semitism. If the Mosaic Law was obsolete, then the Law must be bad, and those unenlightened, narrow-minded Jews who insist on keeping it must be bad. Most of us would be horrified to read the history of how Christians have treated Jews from the time they gained political power in the Roman Empire up to the present — on the basis of this theology.

So what did Paul mean? Did Paul not feel guilty when he transgressed the Law? Again, that's the wrong question. In Philippians 3:6, Paul says that he had not transgressed the Law prior to his conversion. In fact, before the Law, he was blameless. Paul apparently experienced none of the useless striving and introspective guilt that so troubled Martin Luther. He did not see the Law as onerous; he had kept every law perfectly since he was 13 years old. For him, it had been the key to salvation.

Paul was not unusual in this assessment. The Jews of his day did not assume that the Law was difficult to follow. The Law was a gift from God and a privilege to obey. Faithful Jews would repeat this blessing as they performed the most minute rule: "Blessed be thou, O Lord, who has sanctified us with thy commandments and has commended us."[1]

The problem, then, lay not in an inability to keep the Law. Rather, it was something much deeper and more insidious, the problem of self-righteousness. What is it that one hopes to get out of keeping the Law? The admiration and envy of others? Special honors in the synagogue, among one's peers, and in the world to come? Paul speaks in 7:5 of how "our sinful

---

1. Jewett, *Romans*, 83.

passions, aroused by the law, were at work in our members to bear fruit for death." Paul knew that his zeal for the Law had indeed wrought death. In that zeal he had assumed that the crucifixion of Jesus was appropriate because he was a criminal. Paul had affirmed the martyrdom of Stephen, a follower of Jesus. Such zeal had driven Paul to persecute any Christian he could find.

Yet on the road to Damascus, Jesus himself had showed Paul that all his passion for keeping the Law was wrong and was actually "bearing fruit for death." Unless he turned about face, he was participating in sin and death. It is this background we must bring to Romans 7. Paul understood both the goodness of the Jewish Law, *and* how sin could twist it into an instrument of death.

But how will this message sit with the Roman Christians? Will those who stress keeping the Law be offended? Will those who think the Law is not important be affirmed in their belief and smirk at the lawkeepers? If they do, is such prideful nonconformity to the Law a new law that also becomes an instrument of sin? The simulation should reveal many different attitudes and opinions.

Romans 7 can be outlined thus:

- The Two Ages and the Law (7:1-6)
- The Problem with the Law (7:7-12)
- Sin and Paul's Conversion (7:13-25)

Understanding the Background

Who Died?

In Paul's analogy of a married woman bound to her husband by Law (7:1-6), Paul does not say that the *Law* died and is worthless in and of itself. Rather, the *believer* has died (*with Christ,* as in Rom. 6), and is now freed from the Law. Even though the Law may be good and valuable in certain ways, believers in Christ are discharged from that Law to become "slaves not under the old written code but in the new life of the Spirit" (7:6).

Paul's Choice of an Analogy

Paul's choice of a woman as the subject of his analogy may tell us something about his view of woman's status in the Roman Empire. Generally, females were married by the age of 18 or even earlier — some at or before the onset of puberty. Males were normally at least ten years older than their wives,[2] and thus the relationship could hardly have been equal in terms of maturity and worldly experience. No wonder wives were told to submit and obey their husbands when the relationship at times must have seemed more like father and daughter than husband and wife.

Further, unless a woman died in childbirth (which many did), she likely outlived her husband and was free to marry again, someone more her own age. These second marriages were more egalitarian because husband and wife had similar age and maturity.[3] By using such an analogy, Paul has chosen an example that the Roman Christians understand. By connecting the believer's freedom from the Law with a woman's freedom from her first, unequal marriage, he tacitly shows his understanding and approval of a more egalitarian relationship.

Who Is the "I" Paul Refers to?

In Romans 7:7-25, Paul moves from using the first-person plural "we" to the first-person singular "I." Much ink has been spilled over the question of who this "I" refers to, whether the description of the conflicted ego refers to Paul (or the Christian in general), before or after conversion. Knowing what we do about the conflict among the Christians at Rome and about Paul's own zeal for the Law which was brought up short on the road to Damascus, we can surmise that Paul is both universal and specific. From his own painful experience he knows how faithfully keeping the Law can lead to self-righteousness and therefore sin and death. But he also knows

2. Saller, "Slavery," 68.

3. John White of Loyola University of Chicago, spoken at a panel presentation of the Chicago Society of Biblical Research on "What Do We Now Know about Women in the Ancient Mediterranean World?" April 4, 1992.

that this is a universal experience. The Christians at Rome are also struggling with self-righteousness, envy, and covetousness.

N. W. Watson notes that the Jewish community would have been used to hearing Scripture read, such as the Psalms, where the first-person singular was used to express a state of mind common to all Israel.[4] James D. G. Dunn sees many allusions to Adam and the Genesis 3 account of the fall in verses 7-11. Thus "I" is more than Paul's particular experience; it is the prototypical experience of Adam. Thus by the time we reach verses 9 and 10, Paul's listeners would surely understand he was talking about Adam, "for only in the case of Adam is it possible to make such a clear distinction between a before-and-after of the Law: before the commandment came, life; after the commandment, sin and death."[5]

Preparing for Simulation

What is the attitude of your character toward the Jewish Law? Are you one of the "weak" who thinks it's important to keep the Law in order to find full salvation? Are you one of the "strong" who sees it as unnecessary? Or are you wishy-washy and not sure what you think, so you keep it as well as possible, just in case it might be important?

Phoebe or Her Secretary Reads Romans 7

Use the NRSV or other available text.

Questions to Discuss in Your House Church

1. What do you as a Jew or a Gentile believe about the Law? Is it necessary for salvation? Discuss this with the others in your house church. What is the range of opinions within your group? For those who do

---

4. N. W. Watson, "The Interpretation of Romans VII," *Australian Biblical Review* 21 (1973): 27-39.

5. Dunn, *Romans 1–8*, 401.

keep all or some of the laws, what might they be, and how do they impact your lives? What happens when you keep the Sabbath? What do you do when you are unable to find kosher meat? Do you circumcise your children? Do you observe ritual purification (Lev. 15)? Do couples avoid sex while the woman is menstruating (Lev. 18:19)? Do you make sure your clothes are not woven from a mixture of fibers (Deut. 22:11)?

2. Have various members of your group verbalize what they think Paul is saying. Do you agree with Paul? How does Paul's view of the Law agree with your view? Do you believe that the Law is holy and spiritual (7:12, 14)? On the other hand, do you believe that the Law arouses sinful passions (7:5)?

3. Do you see evidence of self-righteousness in members of other house churches who keep the Law? Do you see evidence of self-righteousness in members of your own house church who keep the Law? What about those who *don't* keep the Law: do they feel superior because they don't? Might this sense of superiority be another form of self-righteousness and pride?

4. In 7:7-8, Paul refers to covetousness and desire. Dunn notes that the Jews of Paul's day viewed covetousness or lust as the root of all sin (cf. James 1:15).[6] Do you see evidence of covetousness among the house-church groups in Rome? Within your own group? In your own character? Are the poorer Christians coveting the wealth and opportunities of those who have more? Do slaves covet the freedom of others? Is anything wrong with that kind of covetousness?

Debriefing and Applying

Do a brief analysis of your simulation. Did you stay in character? Did you reach any impasse about who was right or wrong among the conservatives or liberals? Were you able to understand the subtlety of sin in the Roman context and see how it might have applied to your character or those in your house church?

6. Dunn, *Romans 1–8*, 400.

1. How can we apply Paul's message to our lives today? Christian churches, and Mennonite denominations in particular, have a history of disagreement and strife over theological, practical, and ethical issues. Most splits within churches happen because of disagreements about lifestyle, behavior, or the observance of certain rules. How does this relate to Paul's message of Romans 7? In such a conflict, whose side would Paul be on?

2. What rules or customs in our culture define how we behave? Are we trapped by the need to keep up with the Joneses and maintain a middle-class lifestyle, by the need to wear designer clothes, by insisting on "politically correct" language and behavior, or any other cultural standards? Are our efforts to resist conforming to certain customs in our society actually a new law of nonconformity? or perhaps conformity to rules that are even more "in" or elite?

3. In light of your discussion of #3 (above), what do you think of Paul's solution that it doesn't matter what law you keep, so long as you understand it will not make you righteous before God? Is it possible that some people have made a new law out of their Christian beliefs and are just as self-righteous as those who reject Jesus as a way of salvation? Is it ever possible to fully pin down the subtlety of sin? What do you think is the solution?

13 | The Christian's Cloud Nine: The Paradox of Suffering and Glory

Romans 8

Of all the chapters in the Bible, Romans 8 is one of the most familiar to us. Sometimes it is too familiar, as when a pious person quotes Romans 8:28, about God working everything out for good — and something bad has happened or someone we love has died and we feel wretched. Sometimes we'd rather *not* hear Romans 8:28, thank you!

Nevertheless, the chapter as a whole is a ringing climax to Paul's second proof (Rom. 5–8) and indeed the high point of the entire letter. If you are in a joyous mood, Romans 8 can transport you to the mountaintop!

Let us think again about our seesaw, with sin and death on one side, and grace and eternal life on the other, and the Law being the fulcrum between them. Now Paul adds another element to each side of the seesaw. *Flesh* joins sin and death on the negative side, and *Spirit* joins life and peace on the positive side. Indeed, it must have been the creativity and power of the Spirit that practically writes this chapter and sets Paul's pen singing with poetry by the time he gets to the "more than conquerors" section.

Because of the break in thought between chapters 7 and 8, it is possible that here Phoebe took a short break in reading as the members of those small house churches gathered around her. I imagine her eyes brightening and her tone lifting as she begins chapter 8, perhaps holding forth in the charismatic style of some African-American preachers, while the congregation joins in with equally fervent responses. "If God is for us, who can be against us" — "NO ONE!"

This chapter, as part of the second proof of Paul's thesis about the power of the gospel, shows further implications of what being rightwised through Christ is all about. When we walk according to the Spirit, we do not walk according to the flesh as before. This life, though full of suffering, leads to glory and the renewal of the entire creation. Robert Jewett outlines it thus (with overlap on 8:17):

- Flesh and Spirit (8:1-17)
    1. Liberation by Christ (8:1-4)
    2. The contrast between flesh and spirit (8:5-9)
    3. The problem of the body (8:10-11)
    4. Spirit and sonship (8:12-17)
- Human Suffering (8:17-30)
    1. Spirit, suffering, and hope (8:17-25)
    2. Human vulnerability and weakness (8:26-27)
    3. Providence and predestination (8:28-30)
- Principalities and Powers (8:31-39)[1]

Understanding the Background

Before you listen to Romans 8 being read, it is helpful to know the ancient Roman meaning of some terms and ideas familiar to us today. How would the earliest Christians have understood this chapter?

Flesh versus Spirit

Recently I heard a speaker mention Paul as an example of someone critical of bodily pleasure and sensuality. She was referring to passages like Romans 8, where Paul uses flesh in a negative way. However, if we stay with our context in Romans 5–8 and our first-century situation of Jew-Gentile conflicts, a far different meaning appears. *Flesh* harks back to circumcised flesh, which some Jews and Judaizing Christians were insisting was necessary for salvation.[2] It also refers to the attitude of self-righteousness and

1. Jewett, *Romans,* 92.
2. Jewett, *Romans,* 93.

ethnic superiority discussed in the previous chapter. When we depend on our own righteousness, we are not depending on the grace of God.

In 8:3, we see that the Law was not powerful enough to overcome this "fleshly" attitude. Its power is only broken through Jesus, who came in the flesh (a clever play on words, since "flesh" here leans more toward simply the human condition — God having to come in the flesh in order to rightwise those who were also in the flesh).

Paul contrasts living according to the flesh with living according to the Spirit, by which he means the Spirit of Christ. Paul was a charismatic who believed that belonging to Christ and having the Spirit are the same thing.[3]

Adoption

In 8:14-17 Paul uses the image of adoption to explain the Christian's relationship to God. We all understand adoption as something that usually happens when a couple cannot have children of their own and they adopt a baby who cannot be raised by the biological mother or parents. In the Roman Empire, however, if an older man did not have a son of his own, he might legally adopt a younger man to inherit his wealth and status. The adoptee may even have been a favorite slave. (Women remained under the legal authority of their father or husband all their lives and did not ordinarily have the right either to inherit or to adopt a son or daughter.)

Such adoption was quite common and was a treasured status. Indeed, many Roman emperors came to the throne through adoption. During Paul's lifetime, the emperor Augustus claimed his right to power through his adoption by Julius Caesar; and Augustus in turn adopted his nephew Tiberius, the next emperor, after the death of the two sons of his only child, a daughter.

But Paul adds a deeper dimension to his use of adoption imagery by portraying God not only as wealthy and generous, but also as loving and personal. God is *Abba,* an intimate term meaning *Daddy* or *Papa.* It is the term Jesus used when praying to God.

---

3. Dunn, *Romans 1–8,* 444.

Resurrection of the Body

In 8:11 and 23, Paul expressly refers to bodily resurrection. This is consistent with the Old Testament Hebrew concept of humanity that never separated body and soul. If one was to be resurrected, it meant the whole person. This contrasts with the Greek idea of the body as a prison from which the soul was freed at death. (Unfortunately, our present religious ideas of "heaven" are more influenced by the Greek concept.)

Ecological Liberation through the Spirit

In 8:18-25, Paul says that, in addition to humans, the entire creation is in bondage to sin and death. Therefore, when the children of God come into their final inheritance, the created world will also be renewed and released from its bondage. As Jewett puts it, "When humans are transformed, the earth itself will be restored as well. Responsibility for the soil will replace exploitation. Destruction of the forests and the waterways of the earth will be replaced by a transformation, as the entire world begins to reflect its intended glory with the rightwising of humans."[4]

Principalities and Powers

The conclusion of chapter 8 can be considered the conclusion of the entire proof of Romans 5–8. All of the powers of sin and death and the flesh and the law, which Paul mentions in 5–8, along with every other power, cannot separate us from the love of God in Christ Jesus.

Much more than now, people of Paul's day believed that there were intermediate powers between God and humans, both good and evil. These powers were often seen as the personification of a nation or an institution. For example, the goddess Roma was the spirit of Rome. When people wanted to build a temple to the emperor Augustus (thus implying he was a

---

4. Jewett, *Romans*, 98.

god), he would only allow this if the temple was also dedicated to Roma.[5] We might also think of the institutions of slavery or the *oikonomia* (the hierarchically structured household economy) as powers that severely controlled people's lives in Paul's day. Thomas N. Finger's systematic theology, *Christian Theology: An Eschatological Approach,* shows how pervasively such powers are assumed and discussed throughout both Old and New Testaments.[6]

Walter Wink has written a trilogy on "the powers" to which the New Testament refers, and he shows how they continue to exist in our modern age.[7] Every organization or entity has a "spirit" or "angel," which is more than the sum of the parts of that organization. It can be good, evil, or neutral. Often intervention by one person or even a group of persons is not powerful enough to change the spirit of an organization or institution. When a new president of the United States is elected, for instance, he soon finds out how hard it is to change the spirit of the Congress!

Paul is saying in 8:38-39 that none of the powers in existence in the universe can "separate us from the love of God in Christ Jesus our Lord." It is significant that Paul uses the word "Lord" (*kurios* in Greek) in this context because it was a political term referring to the one who had supreme power over an entity such as the state. Nero may have been *kurios* of the Roman Empire at that time, but the power of *kurios Christos Iēsous* was greater.

Preparing for Simulation

As a conservative or liberal, Jew or Gentile, think through what kind of suffering you have been enduring. Then reflect on what you have experienced of the Spirit in your life.

---

5. Cary and Scullard, *A History of Rome,* 341.

6. Thomas N. Finger, *Christian Theology: An Eschatological Approach,* 2 vols. (Scottdale, Pa.: Herald Press, 1985-89), 2:84-88, 542 (index).

7. Walter Wink, *Naming the Powers: The Language of Power in the New Testament* (Philadelphia: Fortress, 1984); *Unmasking the Powers: The Invisible Forces That Determine Human Existence* (Philadelphia: Fortress, 1986); *Engaging the Powers: Discernment and Resistance in a World of Domination* (Minneapolis: Fortress, 1992).

Phoebe or Her Secretary Reads Romans 8

I recommend using the NRSV for this chapter, where the use of a pronoun for *the Spirit* is avoided. This avoids choosing feminine gender as with Hebrew *ruakh,* neuter gender as with Greek *pneuma,* or the Western, English use of the masculine gender pronoun for *the Spirit.* Anyhow, gender in grammar is not identical with sexual gender — as in German *das Mädchen* (girl) — and our language for God the Spirit uses metaphor and analogy. In Hebrew, the spirit of any person, male or female, is feminine. By contrast, our Western tradition has tended to see every aspect of God as masculine.

Questions to Discuss in Your House Church

1. As a conservative, do Paul's statements about the flesh offend you? Do you agree with Paul that those who don't keep the Law are not condemned (8:1-4)?

2. Who in your house church or among the other house churches do you think has the mind of the flesh (8:5-8)? Do you think Paul is commenting on the conflict that exists between and among the house churches?

3. What do you think will happen to your body? Will it be resurrected at the end of time (8:11, 23), or is only the soul immortal? How does Paul's view of bodilyness compare with that taught in your previous religion?

4. Paul clearly is a charismatic who refers to ecstatic experiences in the Spirit (8:15-16, 26-27). How do you feel about that as a Jew? as a Gentile in a house church that tends to be charismatic?

5. If you are a woman, what do you think of Paul's use of the male image of adoption? Can daughters inherit in God's realm? In 8:14, the Greek word is "sons," but in 8:16 Paul changes to the word "children." Is that significant?

6. Do you agree with Paul's hope for the future? From your vantage point, how do you see the creation groaning and in bondage to decay (8:21)? Are there environmental problems such as pollution of the

Tiber River? garbage in the streets? overcrowding? crime? forced labor? unjust taxation? epidemic illnesses? difficulties and death in childbirth? What kind of hope do *you* have for the future?

7. Who is included in the "predestined" (8:28-30)? Those critical conservatives? Those licentious liberals? Only your house church?

8. What powers and principalities do you fear in this world?

9. What is your overall reaction to the tone of this chapter? Is Paul inspiring, or too idealistic?

Debriefing and Applying

Follow the debriefing suggestions from previous chapters. Then use these questions to help apply Paul's message to our lives today.

1. What is the Christian hope today? Paul believed in the bodily resurrection of the dead and the renewal of all creation. Is such a hope realistic and believable in our day, especially since it hasn't happened for almost 2,000 years? Is bodily resurrection consistent with our common statements about "going to heaven when we die" and our souls floating around without bodies?

2. Do Paul's remarks about the decay and futility of creation have any relationship to our environmental problems today? Are these problems worse than they were in Paul's day? If so, how? Do you agree with Paul that this earth itself will be renewed when God's children are fully liberated?

3. In our "scientific" age, do principalities and powers still exist? What forms might they take today? Do social forces such as nationalism or materialism, social institutions like the military or big business, or forms of government — socialism, capitalism, totalitarianism, etc. — have a life of their own that exercises power over individuals and groups? If so, how can we interpret Romans 8:31-39 today?

4. If setting the mind on the Spirit is life and peace, what does this say about hostility between Christians or groups of Christians today?

What attitudes should we take toward Christians with different beliefs or lifestyles than ours?

5. How do you personally understand Romans 8:28? How do you experience God's work in your own life?

6. What is your experience with the sort of charismatic emphasis Paul describes, such as in 8:15-16 and 26-27?

14 | Tell Us the Truth, Paul — Has the Word of God Failed?

Romans 9–11

After the magnificent crescendo of Romans 8, another break in the reading of Paul's letter follows. By now sweat streams down the face of the reader while finishing Paul's second proof in the hot little room where the congregation is gathered. The listeners applaud, some breaking out in tongues. A hymn of praise is sung, while babies wake up and need to be fed. Some go outside to the "bathroom."

"I got the part about being children of God," a wiggly youngster might have said. "Now is it over?"

"Oh no," answers the parent, understanding better the nature of formal speeches. "I think Paul has more to tell us. Besides, I don't think he's made it clear enough yet why he's gone to all this trouble to write us this letter."

In spite of the jubilation of the past section of Paul's speech, and the upbeat message of "no condemnation" throughout the whole proof, an undercurrent of uneasiness must be running through the hearts of some listeners at this point, as they think:

Sure, this must be good news for the Gentiles and those liberal Jews who are forsaking their sacred laws. Let them sing their charismatic hymns and speak in wild tongues! But with all this talk of God's grace and acceptance apart from the Law, has Paul really sold out his Jewish birthright? Has he cut himself off from his own brothers and sisters? Has he betrayed the faith of his ancestors and ignored the fact that Jesus came as the Messiah of Israel? Is he trying to win over all these Gentiles because he thinks the word of God in the Holy Scriptures has *failed*? And what does this mean for my relatives who still faithfully attend the synagogue up the street and observe God's covenant?

As a conservative Jew, you are deeply troubled by this. Paul did try to reassure you in 3:1-2. He still uses a lot of quotes from Scripture. But his view of Moses' Law still seems rather negative. You are worrying that Paul means to repudiate the Jewish Law altogether and negate your heritage, your traditions, and your lifestyle. Unless he deals with these issues more adequately in the latter part of his speech, you will be angry and definitely not encourage him to visit Rome.

Romans 9–11 deals with exactly the questions which concern conscientious Jewish Christians of Paul's day. If Paul is right about the gospel, does that mean that the word of God that came to Israel for many centuries was wrong? Paul's response in these three chapters shows a great deal of struggle over the issues, but his answer is a resounding NO, as we shall see.

For a long time, Romans scholars did not see chapters 9–11 as integrally related to the rest of the letter. Those from a Lutheran tradition, who saw the purpose of Romans as teaching justification by faith, had a hard time making any connection. Why all the big fuss about *Jews?*

But in reconstructing the original situation among the Roman Christians, and in understanding the rhetorical structure of the letter, many pieces of the puzzle fall into place. This is Paul's third proof of his original thesis about the gospel. Here is where he deals at length with the big problem that the first eight chapters have brought into focus: if salvation through Christ is a free gift for Gentiles as well as Jews, then what is the use of the Law? Why bother being an observant Jew?[1]

Following is the outline Jewett suggests for this third proof of Paul's thesis.

- Introduction (9:1-5)
- Election and Israel's Fate (9:6-18)
- Individual Responsibility (9:19-29)

1. A parallel example may be modern feminism. When feminism began to emphasize that women could do more than keep house, raise children, and do volunteer work, some older women who had done only that rejected feminism because they felt that it negated what had given purpose to their lives. They needed a feminist equivalent to Paul writing Romans 9–11!

- The Doctrine of Unenlightened Zeal (9:30–10:4)
- Righteousness by Faith Alone (10:5-13)
- The Rejection of the Gospel (10:14-21)
- God Did Not Reject Israel (11:1-10)
- Why Israel Rejected the Gospel (11:11-24)
- The Mystery of Israel's Salvation (11:25-32)
- Conclusion (11:33-36)[2]

Understanding the Background

In the first section (9:1-5), we see that Paul is speaking to the very objections people had about him. He loves his Jewish brothers and sisters and could even wish himself accursed if it would mean their salvation. Paul may be alluding here to the Jewish idea of one person becoming a martyr in order to save a whole nation, like Moses had suggested about himself to Yahweh in Exodus 32:32.[3] In Romans 9:1-5, Paul seems to be responding to doubts and questions many Jewish Christians had about him and his understanding of the gospel.[4]

God Doesn't Sound Very Fair

The next two sections (9:6-18 and 9:19-29) are hard to understand outside of their context. Several years ago when I was working on a writing assignment dealing with Romans, my father-in-law, not a regular Bible reader, dutifully read Romans in order to be able to talk about it with me. When he got to the part about God loving Jacob and hating Esau (9:8-13) and God hardening the heart of Pharaoh, he quit reading in disgust. He was repulsed by the thought of God condemning one person before birth, who did not even have a chance to do good or evil. What kind of a God would

2. Jewett, *Romans*, 103-104.

3. For this and other suggestions, see Dunn, *Romans 9–16*, 525.

4. Paul Minear in *The Obedience of Faith: The Purpose of Paul in the Epistle to the Romans* (London: SCM, 1971), 73, attempts to reconstruct these criticisms.

not play fair and give everyone an equal chance at a good life? What kind of sadistic God would deliberately harden someone's heart so they *couldn't* do right?

Yet this is not Paul's point at all. Here he is contrasting children of the flesh with children of the promise. He is saying the same thing he said in his first proof in Romans 1–3, that it's not really important who your parents were and whether or not you came over on the *Mayflower* and have a blue-blooded pedigree. God chooses people quite apart from standards humans use to select who is important and worthwhile and who isn't.

In a human sense, Esau the firstborn should have been the chosen son. By human standards, Pharaoh was the most powerful human being in the known world of his day — and the Hebrews were insignificant slaves. But God's choices are not always what we expect. They relate much more to God's promise and the faithful response to that promise than to the "flesh" — our biological ancestors.

Beginning at 9:6, God's point of view is represented. From a human viewpoint, we can say that Jacob and Esau themselves made choices which led to their respective destinies. And Pharaoh was hardening his own heart (Exod. 7:22; 8:15; 9:35; 13:15). But all that is beyond Paul's point: mercy comes from God alone and not from human effort or from the "proper" biological descent.

Because God is free to choose, says Paul in 9:24, God can call not only Jews but also Gentiles. In 9:25-26 Paul uses a quotation from Hosea to underline how things can change, how those who were not the people of God can become God's people. He follows with a quote from Isaiah 10:22-23 that even though there are many children of Israel, only a remnant will be saved.

The Blind Zeal of Israel

In 9:30–10:4, Paul returns to his point in Romans 7:7-25, that many Jews made the same mistake he had. They have been zealous for what they thought was the righteousness of God, only to stumble because they were actually performing works of self-righteousness. Paul may be thinking of examples of nationalistic zeal from Israel's history, such as Phineas lynching a Hebrew man and his consort, a woman from a pagan religion (Num. 25:10-13); or of Mattathias, who killed a Jew who offered sacrifice on the altar of a pagan deity (1 Macc. 2:23-26).

But Paul would also have been thinking of the contemporary scene. Everyone in his Roman audience knew about Jewish Zealots who even then were taking up arms to protest the Roman occupation of Palestine. Several serious incidents had already occurred. Though Paul did not know the outcome of that strife, we know that in 70, about twelve years after he wrote to the Roman Christians, the Zealots provoked Rome into counterattacking. The Jewish-Roman war was ended by the Roman army invading Jerusalem and utterly destroying the temple, thus changing Judaism forever.

Such zeal had been Paul's style as well; for the sake of his religion, he persecuted Christians as far north as Damascus in Syria. But when he met Jesus Christ, he saw that his zeal for God was entirely misplaced. That same zeal had led to the killing of God's Son. The murder of Jesus showed up national zeal for what it was — an attempt to establish self-righteousness and not God's righteousness (10:3). Its result was the opposite of God's will.

By Faith Alone

Romans 10:5-13 contains verses often memorized by evangelicals eager to win converts to Christ. All you have to do to be saved is believe in Jesus and confess him with your mouth. But in light of Paul's later instructions in Romans 12–13 for living a holy life, this text only makes sense in light of what has come before. "By faith alone" must be seen, not as a contrast to ethical and holy living, but as the opposite of performing the zealous works of nationalist violence to which Paul has just referred. With his repeated use of the word "heart," Paul stresses an inner transformation, a thorough embracing of Jesus as the one who brings peace and not hostility.

To make his case stronger, Paul appeals again to Scripture, this time Deuteronomy 30:12-14, to show that even in Judaism the emphasis is on the right attitude of the heart and not simply on one's outer works.

Has God Rejected Israel?

In Romans 11, Paul again asks the scary question: Has God rejected Israel? Absolutely not — for two reasons.

First, already there is a remnant who have accepted Christ, thus showing they are saved by God's grace. Second, even though most of the Jews have so far rejected Christ, this has inadvertently opened the door for the Gentiles to come in. Jewett notes that Paul may be referring to events recorded in the book of Acts. When Jews in Jerusalem began to persecute their fellow Jews who had become Christians, those believers fled to other cities and began preaching there. Thus began the mission to the Gentiles.[5] Later, in a number of cities where Paul preached in the synagogues, Jews threw him out and he then went to the Gentiles.

A Warning to the Gentiles

Beginning in 11:13, Paul speaks directly to the Gentiles among his audience, using the image of an olive tree, highly valued in the Middle East. "Beware," he says. "You are like a wild olive shoot that has been grafted in because some of the original branches were broken off. If you become proud of your new status, you will fall into the same trap as the Jews before you, and your branches will be cut off the tree."

A Mystery Revealed

Paul regards the hardening of the Jews until the full measure of the Gentiles come in as a mystery which is now being revealed (11:25-32). Although his listeners would be familiar with the mystery cults in Rome, that is not the meaning to which he refers. Initiates of those mysteries pledged to keep their knowledge secret from everyone who was not initiated.

But James Dunn says that Paul does not use the vocabulary of the pagan mysteries. He has a Jewish apocalyptic understanding, which sees "mystery" as a secret which God has kept until now, in the last days, when

5. Jewett, *Romans*, 114.

God reveals it to all.[6] This mystery is the mystery of God's purpose in bringing in the Gentiles along with the Jews — and that in the end all Israel will be saved.

In spite of the fact that this mystery is now revealed, Paul closes with a prayer to the God who is still full of mystery, whose mind is so far beyond ours that we cannot plumb its depths.

Preparing for Simulation

Be clear in your mind about your conservative or liberal orientation regarding Jews and Gentiles. Follow carefully the argument of Romans 9–11 when it is read, so you will be able to discuss whether or not Paul makes sense to you and whether his words are valid.

Phoebe or Her Secretary Reads Romans 9–11

Introduction: Israel's Unbelief (9:1-5)

"I am speaking the truth in Christ. . . ."

Election and Israel's Fate (9:6-18)

"It is not as though the word of God had failed. . . ."

Individual Responsibility (9:19-27)

"You will say to me then. . . ."

The Doctrine of Unenlightened Zeal (9:30–10:4)

"What then are we to say? . . ."

---

6. Dunn, *Romans 9–16*, 678.

Righteousness by Faith Alone (10:5-13)

(For oral reading use condensed version in this paragraph.)

"Moses writes concerning the righteousness that comes from the law, that 'the person who does these things will live by them.' But the righteousness that comes from faith says, . . . 'If you confess with your lips that Jesus is Lord and believe in your heart that God raised him from the dead, you will be saved. . . . For there is no distinction between Jew and Greek; the same Lord is Lord of all and is generous to all who call upon him."

The Rejection of the Gospel (10:14-21)

(Here is Paul's plug for his mission.) "But how are [people] to call on one in whom they have not believed? . . ." (read orally at least through 10:17).

God Did Not Reject Israel (11:1-10)

"I ask, then, has God rejected his people? . . ." (read orally at least through 11:7).

Why Israel Rejected the Gospel (11:11-24)

"So I ask, have [the Jews] stumbled so as to fall? . . ."

The Mystery of Israel's Salvation (11:25-32)

"So that you may not claim to be wiser than you are, brothers and sisters. . . ."

Conclusion (11:33-36)

"O the depth of the riches and wisdom and knowledge of God! . . ."

Questions to Discuss in Your House Church

1. As a house church, see if you can articulate Paul's reasoning about why the word of God has not failed. What does Paul see as the value of his Jewish heritage? the present and future role of all the Jews?

2. If you are a conservative Jew, how do you feel now about Paul's discussion of your Jewish heritage? Has he reassured you that you can still be a Jew and a Christian? How does it make you feel to be part of the remnant of Israel that is saved?

3. As a Gentile, does it make you feel proud or humble to be part of the wild olive shoot that's been grafted in? Does Paul's language make you feel accepted on a par with the Jews? inferior to them? superior to them?

   How do you feel about Paul's constant use of Scripture? Do you agree with Paul in his understanding of God's plan for both Jews and Gentiles? Will it make a difference in the way you treat those who keep the Law in your house church — or the Jewish refugees who do not yet have a church to belong to?

4. In the NRSV, Romans 10:4 says that "Christ is the end of the law." The Greek word *telos* translated "end" can also mean "goal" or "fulfillment." Which translation do you prefer? What fits best with Paul's aim of unity in the Roman house churches?

Debriefing and Applying

Follow the debriefing suggestions from previous chapters. Then use these questions to help apply Paul's message for today.

1. Which aspects of Romans 9–11 concern only the first century, and which are relevant for today?

2. What do you think should be the relationship of Jews and Christians today? Do you think Paul would approve of the existence of the state of Israel? of their settlements in the Occupied Territories? How

might our understanding of Romans affect our opinions about Jewish nationalism or Zionism today?

3. How do you think Paul would feel about the "Jews for Jesus" movement?
4. If Paul were alive today, what human groupings might he use instead of Jews and Gentiles? Are you a part of any group where the "old guard" is being threatened by those with different cultural backgrounds or values or lifestyles? Where do you fit in? What are the present tensions? How may Paul's message in Romans 9–11 lessen the tensions and promote unity?
5. How does Romans 10:9-10 fit with the life of holiness discussed in Romans 6?
6. Do the concepts of grace and election bear any relationship to modern questions about hereditary or environmental causes of behavior? Are those raised in a deprived and abusive environment responsible if they in turn become cruel and abusive? How does God's grace work in these situations? Or do our sociopsychological understandings of human behavior eliminate the need for a concept of God at all? Is Paul attributing to God what are actually social forces within society? Are there different ways of looking at the same phenomena?
7. How does Romans 9–11 relate to the need for world mission today?
8. How has God's grace worked in your personal life (if it has)? How do you feel about proclaiming the gospel to others?

Note: If there is time and opportunity, watch "The Dividing Wall," a 23-minute DVD by Mennonite Central Committee, about the 16-foot high wall the Israelis are putting up between themselves and the Palestinians. Would Paul support the Christian Zionist movement, in which some Christians defend the Jews' right to Palestinian land because of the way they interpret Old Testament prophecies? If so, would he care how they treat the Palestinians? Information about obtaining the DVD is available at www.mennonitechurch.ca/resourcecentre/ResourceView/18/6318.

15 | Living in Love —
Ethics for Christian Communities

Romans 12–13

As a high school teenager, I had an unexpected Damascus-Road experience after a friend dragged me, unwilling, to a meeting of conversational prayer with other teens. Though for a long time I could not put into words the wild joy consuming me, the most immediate result was my realization that it was time to stop avoiding washing dishes. I hated housework and used my school assignments as an excuse to avoid it. Encountering the risen Jesus meant a behavior change in the most down-to-earth, nitty-gritty sphere of my life.

A Lutheran couple, now close friends of mine, joined our Mennonite church because they needed support in their stand on nonviolence. This conviction was put to the test when the husband, an engineer, was job-hunting and received an offer from a company doing some contracting for the U.S. military. He brought this matter to our church for counsel and was able to make a decision his conscience — and ours — could live with. Another friend, a freelance technical writer, recently joined our church. One of her first decisions was to give up a lucrative contract she had with General Dynamics, whose primary business is related to the military.

With Romans 12, Paul begins the fourth and last proof of his thesis — that the gospel is the power of God for salvation to both Jews and Greeks, that living *by faith* means *living* by faith. We have noticed Paul's diplomatic skill in persuading his hearers that they are all part of the one people of God, with no differentiation between Jews and Gentiles. His second proof shows them how ethics is to flow naturally from their rightwising and initiation into the body of Christ. Now he gets to specifics — the dishwashing of hospitality, showing love rather than violence to one's enemy, renouncing critical judgment on another person's behavior. Are Paul's listeners prepared to accept his strong words? As you role-play one of these Roman Christians, can you swallow what Paul is telling you?

According to our rhetorical outline, this fourth proof is also divided into ten subsections. However, this lesson will only concern the first six.

- The Theme of the Section (12:1-2)
- The Use of Christian Gifts (12:3-8)
- The Struggle between Good and Evil (12:9-21)
  1. Guidelines for genuine love (12:9)
  2. Life in the congregation (12:10-13)
  3. Life outside the congregation (12:14-20)
  4. Conclusion (12:21)
- Christians and Government (13:1-8a)
- Love and the End Times (13:8b-10)
- Moral Alertness in the Final Days (13:11-14)
- Guidelines for the Weak and Strong (14:1-12)
- Guidelines for Mutual Upbuilding (14:13-23)
- Accepting Outsiders (15:1-6)
- Summary Statements (15:7-13)

Understanding the Background

There are a number of social and political aspects of life in first-century Rome that will help this text come alive and enable us to move into our character roles.

What Kind of Sacrifice?

All the major religious and philosophical systems of the Middle East recognized the need for practical guidance for daily life — how to cope with the unexpected and the frightening, how to deal with power and powerlessness. Ritual helped establish group identity and speak to these needs.[1] For a Jew, the Torah provided both the ethics and the ritual for their way of life.

But now Paul is articulating a redefinition of the people of God as both Jews and Gentiles in one unified body. The same boundary markers of circumcision, Sabbath observance, dietary restrictions, and the sacrificial system are no longer valid for every Christian. What rituals and behaviors should now take their place?

This is why Paul uses the language of sacrifice in 12:1-2. Instead of an offering of animals, the Roman Christians were to give their own bodies in the most practical ways to promote love — first within their own Christian community, and then outward to society, even to their enemies. Their everyday behavior is to be a sacrifice, a new ritual in place of the old.

Zealotry and Vengeance

Politically, it was tough being an ordinary Jew in the first century. We have already learned about the precarious history of Diaspora Jews within the city of Rome. Back in Palestine, the Jews have been paying taxes to Rome since 63 B.C., but in A.D. 6, Judea became a province of the Empire and experienced a census and direct Roman rule.[2]

The common people were harshly oppressed during this time, while some Jewish religious and political leaders sought to accommodate to Roman rule, often lining their own pockets in the process. Though some Jewish protests against Roman arrogance and idolatry were peaceful, various Zealot groups would arise with messianic promises and calls for violent revolution. Such resistance was a direct political affront to the Roman claim to world dominion, and anyone arrested on charges of making "messianic claims" (such as Jesus) or for Zealotry was put to death.[3]

---

1. Dunn, *Romans 9–16*, 715-716.

2. David M. Rhoads, *Israel in Revolution 6-74 C.E.: A Political History Based on the Writings of Josephus* (Philadelphia: Fortress, 1976), 47.

3. Martin Hengel, *Victory over Violence: Jesus and the Revolutionists* (Philadelphia: Fortress, 1973), 44; chapters 3–7 deal with this entire period and its political unrest and violence.

In 44, Galilee, Perea, and Samaria also became provinces of Rome,[4] and during the 50s, violence and apocalyptic messianism escalated.[5] The worse the situation became in Palestine, the more precarious was the political status of Jews in Rome. Already in 49, many were expelled for rioting. Only because Nero was more pro-Jewish than Claudius had Jews been able to drift back to the capital city. But they had no doubt suffered much as refugees, and even those who stayed in Rome by escaping notice of the authorities were obliged to keep a low profile.

In this touchy political situation, Paul counsels non-retaliation (12:19). Jewish Christians with Zealot tendencies for revenge could endanger not only themselves but the Gentiles with whom they were to be united in one church. Though Paul recognizes that it may not always be possible to get along with everyone in society (12:18), he promotes the same radical solution to violence that Jesus first taught — not a cringing subservience but a proactive choice to love one's enemies and do good to them.[6]

Taxes and Revenues

The Roman emperors had no grand scheme of taxation to support the Empire. Theirs was primarily a method of trial and error, seeing how high they could raise taxes and still remain popular.[7] Typically, each would begin his reign by lowering the rate of some particular levy. When taxes became burdensome to a particular populace, there were several approaches.

1. A public spokesman or embassy could plead for the taxes of a particular city to be lowered.
2. Armed rebellion. This was quite common during the first century, less so later.

---

4. Rhoads, *Israel in Revolution*, 68.
5. Rhoads, *Israel in Revolution*, 68-82.
6. Hengel's *Victory over Violence* demonstrates the uniqueness of Jesus' nonviolent approach in a situation of foreign domination that parallels the experience of many in our world today.
7. Ramsay MacMullen, "Tax-Pressure in the Roman Empire," *Latomus* 46 (1987): 737.

3. Flight or secession. People would actually move from one area to another when they could not pay their taxes.

4. Local magnates or leaders are recorded as having contributed large sums of money to their cities in order to ease the tax burden.[8]

When Paul writes to the Romans, another tax protest is in process. There are persistent complaints against companies levying indirect taxes, as well as against tax collectors who overcharged to enrich themselves.[9] Paul uses the same terms for the taxes then being resisted: "taxes"; and "revenue," a form of customs duties.[10] Paying taxes brings one in contact with government officials. Protesting would negatively raise the public profile of the house churches and render the Jews more vulnerable than ever. Arguments over paying taxes would no doubt drive deeper divisions between the Roman Christians, especially since those of the households of Aristobulus and Narcissus may have financial responsibilities in the government.

Peace prevails in most parts of the Empire at this time, and Paul counsels general submission to the government. Nero, the present emperor, has not yet deteriorated into lawlessness and mental illness. Years later, the viciously persecuted Christian communities out of which the book of Revelation emerged have a far more negative view of government than did Paul in 57.

When we understand the specific political situation Paul is addressing, we can see how risky it is to draw universal principles from his statements in 13:1-7. Paul has in mind his grand missionary plan to take the gospel to Spain, and for that he needs a unified church in Rome, as well as a peaceful Empire throughout which he and fellow missionaries can travel and work.

8. MacMullen, "Tax-Pressure in the Roman Empire," 738-739.

9. "Publicani," in *Oxford Classical Dictionary* (London: Oxford University Press, 1949), 747.

10. Jewett, *Romans*, 129.

Benefactors

During the last decade or so, scholars have begun investigating the system of benefaction which, since Homer's Greece in 700 B.C., prevailed throughout the period of the Roman Empire. It sheds light on many New Testament phrases and concepts. Originally the Greek term for "exceptional merit" was formally expressed to rulers or deities who had shown military prowess on behalf of their land or city. They were called benefactors or "saviors," and civic decrees recognizing them were incised on stone and set along the streets of the city they had helped.[11]

Later, the tradition was taken over by clubs and societies *(koinōnia)* as well as in the public sphere. "Exceptional merit" was recognized for gifts other than military might. It could refer to a material gift such as grain to help feed those in the city or money for tax assistance, or even to the teaching of philosophers. With the new interpretation of benefaction, even women and slaves could potentially contribute as benefactors to the welfare of humanity.[12]

This understanding and practice of benefaction was taken over by the Christian communities of the Greco-Roman world, and there are many references to it in the New Testament. On the highest level, God's Son Jesus Christ was the great Benefactor and Savior of all who accepted his gift with gratitude.

Words used in inscriptions to describe such a benefactor are "noble and good" or "righteous and good." A benefaction was called "good." In 13:3, Paul tells the Roman Christians to "do the good (deed) and you shall have praise from the (civil) authority." Evidence from inscriptions shows that rulers *did* praise and honor such benefactors, and also promised to publicly honor those who would do similar benefactions in the future. Literary sources show that great importance was attached to showing gratitude for the gift.[13] Indeed, showing gratitude was considered an obligation; failure to do so was seen by some as a sin.[14]

11. Frederick Danker, *Benefactor* (Chicago: Clayton Publishing House, 1982), 26.
12. Danker, *Benefactor,* 27.
13. Winter, "The Public Honouring of Christian Benefactors," 87-90.
14. Winter, "The Public Honouring of Christian Benefactors," 91.

Thus Paul is encouraging the Roman Christians (at least those who can afford it) to give benefactions in the public arena. The Christians should be well-respected in the city for their good deeds and not their evil deeds (what the city rulers would have called tax resistance). In this way, the civil rulers become "God's servant for your good" (13:4), and Paul's missionary venture can be furthered.

This use of the term "good" can also explain Romans 5:7, where Paul allows that perhaps for a "good person" (a great benefactor) one would dare to die.[15]

Other Political Considerations

Since most or all of us have lived under governments that are to some degree nominally Christian and hold at least theoretically to democratic values, it may be hard to project ourselves back into a pre-Christian world ruled by pagan powers. The following two points should be kept in mind.

First, the Roman government was thoroughly pagan and thoroughly undemocratic. The idea of universal democracy in the political sphere was not developed until the eighteenth century (and is said to have its roots in the inclusiveness of earliest Christianity). Any thought of trying to improve the government through applying Christian principles could not and would not have entered the mind of Paul or of any other Christian leader at least until the age of Constantine after A.D. 325.[16]

Second, "the sword" in Romans 13:4 refers to the government's police and judicial functions within a state, not to its making war with another state.[17] In any case, few Christians at that time would have qualified

15. Winter, "The Public Honouring of Christian Benefactors," 93.

16. For further theological reflection on the Christian's relation to the state, note the emphasis on God as the highest authority in Romans 13:1, 4, 6. See John Howard Yoder in *The Politics of Jesus* (Grand Rapids: Eerdmans, 1972), 193-214; *The Christian Witness to the State,* Institute of Mennonite Studies Series, no. 3 (Faith & Life Press, 1964), 74-77; and *Christian Attitudes to War, Peace, and Revolution* (3003 Benham, Elkhart, Ind.: Co-op Bookstore, 1983), 448-454.

17. Yoder, *The Politics of Jesus,* 205-206.

for military service, since it was a hereditary privilege of the upper classes or of Roman citizens. The *vigiles* were a paramilitary fire brigade and police force for Rome. They were drawn from freedmen and commanded by an officer of equestrian rank.[18] As slaves and foreigners, few first-century Roman Christians would have been eligible for any police, fire, or military involvement.

Reveling and Debauchery

The works of darkness to which Paul refers in 13:13 have specific first-century connotations. "Revelry" was originally a festal procession in honor of Dionysus, the god of wine, and carries the overtone of uninhibited excess.[19] "Debauchery and licentiousness" relate to sexual excess, promiscuous sexual behavior. Romans placed little value on sexual abstinence. Men of higher classes normally did not marry until their late 20s or early 30s. They visited prostitutes or bedded down with any male or female slave who caught their fancy.[20] Jewish laws, however, were much more strict.

"Quarreling and jealousy" can refer to both the frictions within the house churches and in Roman society. In a status-conscious culture like Rome, quarreling characterizes people who dominate others. Jealousy characterizes those who would like to dominate but cannot.[21]

Preparing for Simulation

Before Phoebe reads the text, be clear about your own spiritual gifts, what you think about revenge and loving enemies, how you feel about taxes. Do you tend to be on the liberal side when it comes to reveling and drunkenness (13:13), or more conservative and perhaps more prone to quarreling or

18. Everett Ferguson, *Backgrounds of Early Christianity*, 42.
19. Dunn, *Romans 9–16*, 789.
20. Saller, "Slavery," 68.
21. Jewett, *Romans*, 131.

jealousy? How does being a Jew or Gentile, rich or poor, slave or free, make a difference in how you hear this text?

Phoebe or Her Secretary Reads Romans 12–13

Questions to Discuss in Your House Church

(Choose those most relevant to your group.)

1. What words connect 12:1-2 with the three previous proofs? How do you feel about using one's body as a sacrifice instead of offering animal sacrifices, as in Judaism or other religions? Does that satisfy your need for ritual?

2. In 12:3-8, are the "weak" (conservatives) and the "strong" (liberals) feeling superior to each other in behavior and lifestyles? How are spiritual gifts working out in your house church? Is there a good mix? Is each gift supportive of the others?

3. In 12:13, Paul tells those already living in Rome to extend hospitality to the "saints" (returning Jewish Christians). As a Gentile, how do you feel about that, especially if you are poor and live in a tiny apartment? How do the returning Jews feel?

4. Those of you of higher status, do you "associate with the lowly" (12:16)? Do you live peaceably with everyone, Christian or non-Christian? How do you feel about loving and doing good to your enemies? If you are a Jew, do you want revenge for your expulsion from Rome?

5. How do you feel about Paul's view of the government in 13:1-8a? How may issues of taxes impact on the cell groups in the households of Aristobulus and Narcissus? If paying taxes and revenues will help the exiles stay out of political trouble, will you do it? Under what circumstances would you protest paying taxes?

6. Are you involved in any "works of darkness" listed in 13:11-13? As a liberal, do you agree that things like reveling actually *are* works of

darkness? As an upper-class person or house-church leader, can you serve without dominating others and quarreling? As a slave or lower-class person, are you jealous of those above your station? Is Paul asking you to change *your* lifestyle? If he is, how do you feel about that? Do you share Paul's belief in the imminent return of Jesus?

Debriefing and Applying

Share with the other groups what your house church discussed and concluded. Did you stay in character? What did you learn from the simulation?

1. If we are made right with God by God's grace, then where is the place of ethics? Lutherans have tended to downplay the connection of ethics with grace; Anabaptists see them as inseparable. What do you think is the right balance? Do you base your thinking on Romans?

2. How do the various spiritual gifts balance themselves out in your church congregation? Are all of them equally appreciated?

3. Is the exhortation to love one's enemies practical today? What are the implications? What persons do you know personally who treat you with hostility? In this case, is "love" something you *feel,* or does it mean something you *do* — an active goodwill expressed toward others? How can we express such goodwill toward (a) people we naturally don't like, (b) political "enemies" like Iraq or Iran, (c) those who oppress, exploit, or abuse others, (d) people on both sides of a conflict (such as Israelis and Palestinians)?

4. Through hundreds of years of church history, Romans 13:1-7 has been taken to mean that citizens should never protest against their government but submit to it, regardless. In light of this study on Romans, how would you now interpret the text? How does it fit in the larger ethical context of Romans 12–13? If its message is situational and tied to Paul's missionary goals, what does it mean for our lives today? If we truly try to love our "enemies" by protesting paying taxes to the military, can we justify it by appealing to Romans 12–13?

5. In 13:11-14, Paul connects sober and upright behavior with the sudden, imminent return of Christ. But this did not happen on Paul's time schedule and has not happened yet. Are "works of darkness" also self-destructive on other grounds? Can we make modern analogies with deadly drug and alcohol addictions, sexual promiscuity bringing death by AIDS and other venereal diseases, or materialistic excesses hastening environmental disaster?

16 | How to Get Along When We Don't Agree

Romans 14:1–15:6

Suppose you are part of a church community which takes a fairly liberal and hands-off attitude toward abortion. You assume that women can basically be trusted to make their own choices in the matter and that the decision should be left up to the woman, or if she is married, to the couple. Then suppose a few of your members become persuaded that all abortion is wrong and they begin marching at abortion clinics and pressuring the congregation to start a ministry with pregnant teenagers.

Or suppose you are part of a previously all-white church that begins encouraging racial minorities to join. Several African-American families come, but they are not wholly comfortable with your worship style. As more of them attend, some white folks feel threatened; the church is no longer "theirs." Leadership conflicts develop.

Or suppose you are part of a congregation but receive a call to serve on an overseas mission venture for several years. When you return, the church has changed. People seem more materialistic. They seem more interested in holding square dances and self-help therapy groups in the church building than in evangelism. Some members have started an AIDS support network. You are convinced the church is losing its distinctiveness and becoming too much like "the world." Several other members of the congregation strongly agree with you.

Throughout our simulation study of Romans, we have been moving from more universal ideas to the practical ways they should be worked out. Many times we can agree with an ideal in principle, but when it comes to practicing it in our own lives, we balk. Paul has been moving from the concept of God's total impartiality to both Jews and Gentiles to implications of how that works out in daily life. In 14:1–15:6, Paul presses on sore spots of specific differences in lifestyle among the Roman Christians. How do we get along with each other when we don't agree?

This passage is one of my favorites in Romans, because I see all around me painful results of what happens when Christians disagree with each other. It even happened one time when I led a Romans simulation. My class included people of different religious backgrounds (fundamentalist and Mennonite), and we had a heated discussion over Romans 13 and how we are supposed to relate to the government. This led to further divisions over whether the government should regulate abortion.

I was so grateful that Romans 14 came after Romans 13, so that at our next class we could discuss what to do when we don't agree. Sadly, one woman never returned for that discussion. Later she told me she was too upset to return, since the other Christians in the group didn't agree with her views on abortion and paying taxes. We all grieved over losing this person. Yet it was a living and powerful example to me and to the other members of the class of our need for Romans 14 and our need to know what to do when we don't agree.

Some of the touchiest problems in Roman house churches — what to eat and what holy days to observe — may seem petty to us today. But they were crucial issues at that time, as we shall see when we climb back into the skin of the Roman Christians during our simulation. In the particularities of a situation, we can most easily make connections with our own lives. We wish for more rather than fewer details.

This is the second part of the fourth and final proof of Paul's thesis, the proof that deals with ethics and righteous living. The previous chapter discussed the first six subsections of this proof. Now we look at the next three:

- Guidelines for the Weak and Strong (14:1-12)
- Guidelines for Mutual Upbuilding (14:13-23)
- Accepting Outsiders (15:1-6)
- Summary Statements (15:7-13) will be considered in the next chapter.

Understanding the Background

To understand how important the issues discussed in this section are, we need answers to two questions:

1. The identity of the "strong" and the "weak."
2. Why issues of diet and observing holy days were divisive.

Who Are the Strong and the Weak?

Paul's earlier letter to the Corinthians also talks about the strong and the weak, but in connection with eating meat offered to idols (1 Cor. 8, 10). In Corinth, the "weak" were those with a conscience against eating such meat because of its connection with idolatry. The "strong" were those who believed that since other gods did not exist, it did not matter whether or not the meat had been first offered to an idol in some pagan ritual.

Paul does not mention idols in Romans, so scholars have argued about whether or not he is referring to an actual situation in Rome, or only making an analogy from the Corinthian situation.[1]

Most scholars, especially recently, tend to believe Paul was referring to an actual problem in Rome. The "strong" are Roman Christians who emphasize freedom from the Torah (more likely Gentiles), and the "weak" are (mostly) Jewish Christians who believe it is important to observe Jewish holy days and dietary practices.[2]

But disagreements, as we know, are rarely purely theological, so we must take account of social and political aspects as well. A 1990 disserta-

---

1. One scholar who believes the latter is Robert J. Karris, "Romans 14:1–15:13 and the Occasion of Romans," in *The Romans Debate*, 65-84; originally in *Catholic Biblical Quarterly* 25 (1973).

2. This view goes back as far as Origen (third century) and John Chrysostom (fourth century) through Philipp Melanchthon (sixteenth century), J. J. Wettstein (eighteenth century), E. Riggenbach (nineteenth century), and twentieth-century scholars such as Otto Michel, Robert Jewett, Ernst Käsemann, C. E. B. Cranfield, and Ulrich Wilckens.

tion by Mark Reasoner brings to light some of these influences which help us understand who is "strong" and who is "weak."[3]

First, Reasoner examines the social composition of the city of Rome. "Strong" and "weak" have to do with social status. The "strong," he says, are either Roman citizens or foreign-born people who take pains to live as Roman as possible. They are most likely freedpersons who have risen in status and property holdings above people of their own class, and even above some of the poorer freeborn persons. They exercise authority over those equal to or below them in social status.[4]

The "weak," on the other hand, are foreigners or those who sympathize with foreign religions and cultures (such as Judaism). They are scrupulous in religious observance. They have less property than others of their social class and rank, and they do not exercise authority over those considered by Roman society to be below them in rank.[5]

In a society as ethnically diversified and status-conscious as Rome, ideas of status and power enter Christian cell groups as well, though with variations. "Strong" and "weak" have different lifestyles and rituals, related to one's diet and observance of special days. Though the "weak" are more likely Jewish, other foreigners may have their own varying lifestyles which contribute to the friction.

If indeed the "weak" have less status and power in the church, and fewer privileges in society, they may be thinking more about the eschatological future and God's judgment. They may wonder if the "strong" will survive God's judgment after death, which explains Paul's reassurance in 14:4b and 8b. And if the "strong" were forcing the "weak" to follow their own practices[6] (such as eating anything), the "weak" may also have been worried about God's judgment on themselves.[7] They feel resentful at coercion by the "strong."

3. Mark Reasoner, "The 'Strong' and the 'Weak' in Rome and in Paul's Theology," unpublished Ph.D. dissertation, University of Chicago, 1990. (Now published as *The Strong and the Weak: Romans 14:1–15:13 in Context*, Society for New Testament Monograph Series [Cambridge: Cambridge University Press, 1999].)

4. Reasoner, "The 'Strong' and the 'Weak,'" 219.

5. Reasoner, "The 'Strong' and the 'Weak,'" 220.

6. Reasoner, "The 'Strong' and the 'Weak,'" 134-135.

7. Reasoner, "The 'Strong' and the 'Weak,'" 139-140.

On Eating and Drinking

Both eating meat and vegetarianism are options in first-century Rome. Several emperors at that time, including Claudius and Nero, believe eating meat is not necessary (except for themselves) and forbid taverns to serve it.[8] Some philosophical and religious traditions teach that abstaining from meat is essential for spiritual or cultic purity and that killing animals is evil. Some slaveowners do not serve meat to their slaves. And the poorer one is, the less likely one is to have any meat at all.

Generally, Jews are not vegetarians. But they may not be eating meat if they cannot get kosher butchering. Since Jews were expelled less than 10 years earlier, kosher meat shops may still be closed down. The first-century Jewish historian Flavius Josephus notes that one would need official permission to open such a shop.[9] Jewish Christians returning to Rome in small numbers may not want to call attention to their presence by insisting on properly slaughtered animals and may prefer to avoid meat altogether.[10]

On Observing Holy Days

Several options are possible for what Paul may mean by observing or not observing days. Most obvious is the Jewish Sabbath, in one of the Ten Commandments and a major practice sacred to Jews, distinguishing them from non-Jews. The Romans often scorn such Sabbath observance as idleness or laziness.[11] However, Paul may also have in mind the six annual feasts and seven ceremonial Sabbaths. Beyond a Jewish framework, Gentile superstitions may compel some to observe certain days as a way to protect themselves from supernatural beings.[12]

If the "strong" are more Roman and less foreign in their lifestyle, they will view *all* observing of days — whether Jewish or Gentile — as

---

8. Reasoner, "The 'Strong' and the 'Weak,'" 219.
9. Josephus, *Antiquities* 14.261.
10. Dunn, *Romans 9–16*, 801.
11. Reasoner, "The 'Strong' and the 'Weak,'" 289-290.
12. Reasoner, "The 'Strong' and the 'Weak,'" 266, 284-285.

mere superstition. They will despise the "weak" for their anxiety or concern over this practice.

What Is Paul's Solution?

At bottom, arguing over matters of lifestyle comes down to a power struggle. Those who are "strong" tend to have more power; their response is to despise and scorn the "weak." For their part, the "weak" may be using dietary and calendar laws to judge and condemn the "strong" as a way to exercise limited power. Paul responds by urging the Christians to accept and welcome each other just the way they are, without arguing about it or pressuring each other to change. Amazingly, though he considers himself one of the "strong" without the need to observe the Jewish Law, he does not ask anyone else to stop observing it. Rather, they should listen to their own consciences and call each other to mutual tolerance.[13]

Here Paul uses the Roman concept of "obligation."[14] Thus in any relationship, even of different social status, there is a mutual exchange of goods and services. The response of a socially inferior or less powerful person who receives a gift from a wealthier benefactor may be no more than an expression of thanksgiving and gratitude (see 14:6 on how *all* are to respond thankfully to God as the Great Benefactor). In Romans 14:1–15:13, the obligation on both "weak" and "strong" is to live in mutual dependence on each other since all are indebted to God.

Preparing for Simulation

If you are part of a group doing the simulation, ponder your position as a Jew, Gentile, slave, free, poor or not-so-poor, conservative or liberal: what are your instinctive beliefs and practices on issues of eating meat or obser-

13. For a fuller discussion of this topic, see Robert Jewett, "Guidelines for Tolerant Congregations," in *Christian Tolerance* (Philadelphia: Fortress, 1982), 126-142.
14. Reasoner, "The 'Strong' and the 'Weak,'" 256-273.

vance of holy days? Are you one of the "weak" or the "strong"? How much power and honor do you feel you have in your house church or tenement church? Be prepared to argue your position with others in your group.

Phoebe or Her Secretary Reads Romans 14:1–15:6

Questions to Discuss in Your House Church

What is Paul's main idea in this section? What principles does he offer to deal with lifestyle differences among Christians? Do you agree with Paul's solution? Does it mean that the "strong" should obligate themselves to practice the same rules the "weak" are observing? Are you willing to change any of your behaviors? Which ones? Why or why not? Do you think Paul has no authority to meddle in your business?

How important is mutual upbuilding and harmony to you? Would you rather try to persuade everyone to do things your way? Or do you do what you want regardless of how others feel?

Debriefing and Applying

If you are part of a house-church simulation, take time to discuss the process with the entire group. How well did you stay in character? How strongly did everyone in your group argue for their position and practice? What did your group conclude? What did you learn from the simulation?

1. How far can we go toward applying Paul's principles of Christian tolerance to things on which we disagree today? Will it work for cross-cultural and cross-racial conflicts? How about controversial social issues like abortion, participation in war, or homosexuality?
2. What are points of disagreement within your own church community, your denomination, or even your youth group? Are they related to liberal-conservative power struggles or other power issues? How

willing are you to tolerate different lifestyles within your Christian community?

3. On the other hand, are there limits to tolerance in the Christian community? Are some practices inherently wrong because they are not loving and are not done in honor of Christ — such as wife or child abuse, or alcoholism? If so, what should we do about practices within the Christian community that are abusive and/or exploitative of others?

17 | Eating Together: A Roman Agape Meal

Romans 15:7-13

No doubt all of us are familiar with church potlucks. We enjoy the wide variety of slow-cooker stews and jello salads. Teens and kids don't miss a chance to sample the brownies, cookies, and pies they would never have available all at one time at home. For all of us, eating together is a wonderful way to converse and catch up on each other's lives.

The association of worship, fellowship, and food has a long history. Jesus himself was accused of being a glutton and a wino. Someone has said that in Luke's Gospel, all the stories of Jesus seem to show him either on his way to a meal, eating a meal, or coming from a meal! His last warm memory before the horror of arrest, torture, and execution was the Passover meal with his intimate friends. Christians have reenacted this meal for almost 2000 years and will continue to do so until the end of time — until we eat it together in Jesus' presence in the New Creation.

Once there was no difference between a meal eaten with Christian believers and what we call "communion," sharing the bread and wine of Jesus' body and blood. No doubt the earliest Christians ate together often when they met for worship and fellowship, celebrating with the common food of their day, bread and diluted wine. It was a holy time, often with meager food but in a sense of oneness with each other and the living presence of Christ.

But at other times these events were touched by strife and selfishness and resentment. Though eating together and sharing the Eucharist can draw people together, it can also drive them apart. We know this happened in Corinth, where the wealthy believers refused to share their food with those who had nothing to contribute (1 Cor. 11:20-22). In Rome, food had become a bone of contention (pardon the pun) among the competing Christian cell groups.

143

In a group simulation, you will find it memorable to share the Eucharist and a potluck agape (ä-GÄ-pay) meal (love feast) with all the house-church groups. This can graphically illustrate the continuing rivalry and tension between those who have dietary scruples and those who do not, between those who observe certain holy days and those who do not.

On the other hand, depending on how the simulation in your house church has developed, it could be a time of healing and unified worship. It may also be a time to invite other family members or friends as a way of sharing the excitement of learning through simulation about Paul's letter to the Romans and about the lives of first-century churches. Bringing guests will be most effective, however, if they come as Roman "Jews" or "Gentiles," as slaves or clients of your acquaintance with whom you'd like to share good news. You as a participant will need to educate your guests as to their roles at the meal.

What Foods Not to Bring

Participants should bring one item of food appropriate for their religious convictions, their relative wealth or poverty within their house-church group, and their status within their household as slave, freedperson, or freeperson. The following guidelines should be observed.

If you are a Jew or a Gentile who feels keeping the Law is important:

- Avoid pork, ham, or bacon; rabbit or camel (see Deut. 14:3-8).
- Avoid reptiles or amphibians.
- Avoid mixing meat with dairy products (for example, cheeseburgers and beef stroganoff are out! See Exod. 23:19; 34:26).
- Drain all blood out of meat (see Lev. 17:10-11; Acts 15:20).
- Avoid insects, except locusts (see Lev. 11:20-23).
- Avoid any meat that has been offered to idols.

If you are poor (this would include all or most members of the Saints and Brothers cell groups, as well as poor slaves from other households):

- Bring no meat of any kind. You cannot afford it.
- Bring recipes made from barley, wheat, or lentils. Some of you depend on the government dole, which provides you with a small allotment of wheat and oil.

What Foods Are Appropriate

In addition to the recipes included on the following pages, these foods are also appropriate "as is":

- *Grains:* dark bread, pita bread, wheat crackers, rice, bulgur wheat, lentils (see *More-with-Less Cookbook* for good lentil recipes).[1]
- *Fruits and Vegetables:* cauliflower, asparagus, onions, beans, tomatoes, broccoli, zucchini, eggplant, peppers, okra, cabbage, turnips, olives, dates, lettuce, oranges, grapefruit, grapes, raisins, figs.
- *Dairy:* milk (preferably goat's or camel's milk; cow's milk accepted), cheese, yogurt, cottage cheese, eggs.
- *Beverages:* grape juice (dilute with water if you are poor), wine (usually diluted with two parts water; brought only by those who have no conscience against it).
- *Other:* nuts, seeds, honey.

---

1. Doris Janzen Longacre, *More-with-Less Cookbook* (Scottdale, Pa.: Herald Press, 2000).

Tabooli Salad[2]   *Serves 6-8*

    2 cups bulgur wheat
    8 scallions, very finely chopped
    1 cup fresh parsley, chopped
    3 large firm ripe tomatoes, finely chopped
    1 tablespoon dried mint
    ½ cup olive oil
    3 lemons, juiced
    salt and pepper to taste

Cold Vegetable Mix   *Serves 4*

    1 small eggplant, peeled and cubed
    2 large zucchini, cubed
    1 bell pepper, cut into strips
    2 large tomatoes, seeded and chopped
    2 stalks celery, diced
    1 small hot pepper, dried
    4 tablespoons olive oil
    ½ teaspoon garlic powder
    salt and pepper to taste
    3 tablespoons parsley, chopped
    ¼ cup ketchup
    ½ lemon, juiced

In large skillet lightly sauté vegetables in 4 tablespoons oil.
Add garlic powder, salt, pepper, parsley, ketchup, and lemon juice. Cover
    and simmer 5 minutes.
Allow to cool. Chill and serve.

2. This and the following recipes are from Daniel S. Cutler, *The Bible Cookbook: Lore of Food in Biblical Times Plus Modern Adaptations of Ancient Recipes* (New York: William Morrow, 1985), 92, 94-95, 110, 115, 122, 141-142, 148-149, 167, 189, 197, 203, 220-222, 393; used by permission.

Middle Eastern Cole Slaw   *Serves 4-6*

   3 teaspoons frozen orange juice concentrate, defrosted
   1 lemon, juiced
   3 tablespoons water
   1 teaspoon sugar
   salt and pepper to taste
   ½ tablespoon grated lemon peel
   ½ medium cabbage, shredded

Prepare dressing of orange juice concentrate, lemon juice, water, sugar, salt, and pepper.
Add lemon peel to cabbage. Pour dressing over cabbage, toss, chill, and serve.

Charred Eggplant Salad   *Serves 4*

   1 large eggplant
   4 green peppers, seeded and diced
   2 onions, diced
   1 large clove garlic, crushed
   3 tablespoons olive oil
   2 tablespoons wine vinegar
   salt and pepper to taste

Prick eggplant with fork to prevent explosion in oven. Then, using fork, suspend eggplant in flame of gas stove or lay it directly on electric coils until skin is charred.
Place eggplant on baking sheet and bake in a 450° oven for 60 minutes. Remove and split skin. Pour off bitter brown fluid and allow eggplant to cool.
Scoop out cooled eggplant pulp. Mash with all other ingredients. Chill and serve.

Cucumber Walnut Salad *Serves 4-6*

4 tablespoons olive oil
½ lemon, juiced
1 teaspoon dried mint
⅛ teaspoon sugar
salt and pepper to taste
2 medium cucumbers, peeled and finely diced
1 cup walnuts, chopped
1 green pepper, seeded and finely chopped

Prepare dressing of olive oil, lemon juice, mint, salt, and pepper. Pour over remaining ingredients, toss, and serve.

Spinach Salad *Serves 4*

1 pound fresh spinach
¼ cup plain yogurt
3 tablespoons olive oil
2 tablespoons vinegar
1 teaspoon ground mustard seed
salt and pepper to taste
5 or 6 radishes, sliced
1 hard-boiled egg, sliced

Wash and trim spinach thoroughly, drain, chop coarsely.
Prepare dressing of yogurt, olive oil, vinegar, mustard seed, salt, and pepper. Use this to dress spinach.
Garnish with radishes and hard-boiled egg.

Israeli Breakfast Salad   Serves 4

> 2 large cucumbers, peeled and seeded
> 3 large ripe tomatoes
> 1 scallion
> 1 tablespoon freshly squeezed lemon juice
> 2 tablespoons olive oil
> salt and pepper to taste

Chop vegetables very fine. Toss with dressing, made with rest of ingredients. Chill and serve.

Spiced Cabbage   Serves 4-6

> 1 medium onion, sliced
> 1 medium cabbage, shredded
> 3 tablespoons butter
> salt and pepper to taste
> 1 teaspoon ginger
> ½ cup plain yogurt

Fry onion and cabbage with salt, pepper, and ginger in butter 15 minutes, or until tender.
Dress with yogurt and serve.

Basic Bulgur   Serves 2-3

> 1 cup coarse bulgur wheat
> 2 tablespoons olive oil
> 2 cups meat broth
> salt and pepper to taste

Sauté bulgur in olive oil.
Add seasoned stock, cover, and simmer 30 minutes, or until bulgur is tender.

Spiced Bulgur   *Serves 2-3*

> 1 cup bulgur wheat
> 1 medium onion, finely chopped
> ¼ cup pine nuts
> 4 tablespoons butter
> 3 firm ripe tomatoes, chopped
> ¼ teaspoon coriander
> salt and pepper to taste

Place bulgur in bowl and pour 1 cup boiling water over it. Cover and allow
   to soak 60 minutes.
Sauté onion and pine nuts in 1 tablespoon butter.
Add tomatoes and seasonings. Simmer 5 minutes, adding a little water if
   needed to prevent burning.
Add soaked bulgur and remaining butter. Stir well, heat through, and
   serve.

Yogurt Cheese   *Makes 1¼ quarts*

> 2 quarts plain yogurt
> salt

Pour yogurt into cheesecloth bag and hang from kitchen-sink faucet. Allow
   excess liquid to drain overnight.
Remove cheese next day. Place in serving dish and sprinkle with salt.

Yogurt-Cheese Salad   *Serves 4-6*

> 2 cups Yogurt Cheese (see above)
> 3 scallions, finely chopped
> ½ cup walnuts, chopped
> ¼ cup raisins
> ½ teaspoon dried mint
> 6 radishes, grated
> curly endive or other lettuce leaves

With melon-baller, shape cheese into spheres. Arrange on bed of lettuce leaves.

Mix all but radishes and sprinkle over cheese.

Top with grated radishes and served.

Cold Yogurt Soup II   *Serves 4*

> 2 cucumbers, peeled and seeded
> 3 cups plain yogurt
> ½ teaspoons garlic powder
> ½ teaspoon dried mint
> salt to taste

Chop cucumbers very fine.

Mix yogurt with 1 cup ice water and pour over cucumbers. Add garlic powder, mint, and salt. Stir and serve.

Baked Cheese Squares   *Makes 25*

> 1 cup sharp yellow cheese, grated
> 1 cup flour
> 1 cup milk
> 2 eggs
> salt and pepper to taste

Mix everything in bowl.

Turn into oiled baking dish.

Bake at 325° for 30 minutes, or until lightly browned. Serve as hors d'oeuvres.

Farina Diamonds   *Makes about 25 servings*

> SYRUP
>
> 1½ cups sugar
> 1½ cups water
>
> PASTRY
>
> 6 eggs
> 2½ cups farina (or Cream of Wheat)
> 1 cup chopped nuts
> ½ pound butter, melted

Dissolve sugar in water and bring to boil. Simmer 10 minutes, then set thickened syrup aside to cool.

Beat eggs.

Add farina (or Cream of Wheat), nuts, and melted butter to eggs and stir. Turn out into greased 9-by-13-inch baking pan.

Bake at 350° for 30 minutes. Remove and cut into diamonds. Pour cool syrup over hot farina. Allow to cool and serve.

Lentils and Macaroni   *Serves 2*

½ cup brown lentils
½ pound ground beef
1 medium onion, chopped
¾ cup elbow macaroni
salt and pepper to taste

Simmer lentils in 3 cups salted water 10 minutes.
Brown beef in skillet, then remove with slotted spoon. Sauté onion in fat
until golden brown.
Add macaroni and beef with onion to lentils and cook until macaroni is
tender. Drain. Season with salt and pepper and serve.

Lentils and Squash   *Serves 4-6*

1 butternut, acorn, or hubbard squash
4 tablespoons butter
1 cup brown lentils
salt and pepper to taste
1 large onion, sliced
1 tablespoon lemon juice
½ teaspoon cumin

Halve squash and scoop out seeds. Wash and reserve seeds for later
roasting, or discard. Either peel squash and dice flesh or scoop it out
with melon-baller.
Heat 2 tablespoons butter in skillet. Sauté squash 3 minutes.
Add lentils, salt, pepper, and just enough water to cover. Cover and
simmer 20 minutes, or until tender.
In separate skillet, melt remaining 2 tablespoons butter and fry onion
until golden.
Stir lemon juice and cumin into squash and lentils. Remove to serving
dish. Top with fried onions and serve.

Lentils in Chicken Broth *Serves 2-4*

> 3 tablespoons olive oil
> 1 small onion, chopped
> 1 carrot, chopped
> 1 small stalk celery, chopped
> 1 cup brown lentils
> 1 cup chicken broth
> 1 tablespoon tomato paste
> salt and pepper to taste

Heat olive oil in skillet. Sauté onion, carrot, and celery 3 minutes.
Add lentils and stir in oil.
Add chicken broth, tomato paste, salt, and pepper. Bring to boil and
   simmer 30 minutes, or until tender. Serve hot.

Egg Salad *Serves 4-6*

> 6 hard-boiled eggs
> 1 medium red onion, sliced very thin
> 2 tablespoons olive oil
> ½ lemon, juiced
> ⅛ teaspoon sugar
> salt and pepper to taste
> 1 teaspoon fresh parsley, chopped

Slice eggs and arrange on platter.
Arrange onion on top of eggs.
Prepare dressing of olive oil, lemon juice, sugar, salt, and pepper, and
   pour over salad.
Garnish with chopped parsley and serve.

Sardine Salad   *Serves 2-3*

1 small can sardines

lettuce leaves

1 tomato, chopped

1 small red onion, sliced in rings

⅛ teaspoon ground mustard seed

salt and pepper to taste

1 tablespoon lemon juice

1 hard-boiled egg, sliced

1 tablespoon fresh parsley, chopped

Drain sardines and arrange on bed of lettuce leaves. Cover with tomato and
   onion rings.

Mix mustard seed, salt, and pepper with lemon juice and pour over
   sardines.

Top with egg slices, garnish with chopped parsley, and serve.

Peas and Black Olives   *Serves 4-6*

1 pound green peas

1 small onion, chopped

2 tablespoons butter or olive oil

¼ cup black olives, chopped

¼ teaspoon basil

1 sweet red pepper, chopped, or 3 tablespoons
   pimento, chopped

salt and pepper to taste

Steam peas as in Basil Green Peas (next page).

Sauté onion in butter or olive oil until transparent. Add all other
   ingredients except peas and heat on medium-low heat 5 minutes.

Stir in drained peas and heat 5 minutes. Serve.

Basil Green Peas *Serves 4-6*

1 tablespoon olive oil
2 cups green peas
⅛ teaspoon sugar
salt to taste
¼ teaspoon dried basil

Heat olive oil in a skillet. Sauté peas, making sure each becomes well coated with oil.

Add just enough water to cover. Add sugar, salt, and bring to a boil.
Reduce heat and simmer gently 10 minutes.

Drain. Sprinkle with basil, toss, and serve.

Agape Meal

How should the meal be conducted? I recommend beginning with the Eucharist: diluted wine (or juice) and dark bread. If the total class is quite large, each house church may want to celebrate its own communion. "Phoebe" or another leader can read from 1 Corinthians 11:23-26 the words Paul says he received from the Lord Jesus and has handed on to the churches he founded. I also give each person ahead of time a copy of the meal blessings from the early Christian *Didache* (Teaching). Before sharing the common loaf, read together the "blessing of the broken bread":

> We give you thanks, our Father,
> for the life and knowledge you have made known to us
> through Jesus, your servant.
> Just as this broken bread was scattered upon the mountains
> and then was gathered together and became one,
> so may your church be gathered together
> from the ends of the earth into your kingdom;
> for yours is the glory and the power through Jesus Christ forever.

Before sharing the cup, read together:

> We give you thanks, our Father,
> for the holy vine of David your servant,
> which you have made known to us through Jesus, your servant;
> to you be the glory forever. Amen.

For the meal itself, remember to stay in character and only eat the foods your conscience approves of — unless you want to suffer guilt pangs later! If you are poor and never have opportunity to eat meat, you may be tempted to indulge yourself even at the expense of others. If you are conservative and/or judgmental, keep an eye out for what others are eating and drinking, and be scrupulous yourself. If you have a problem with meat offered to idols, ask those who brought meat if it's "kosher." If you tend to be libertarian and don't care what others think, eat whatever you want —

unless you take to heart Paul's words about not wanting to cause a sister or brother to stumble.

Litany for Close of Agape Meal

The meal can be closed by the following litany from Romans 15:7-13. This is Paul's final effort, at the end of his fourth proof, to draw together the Jews and Gentiles.

Leader: Welcome one another as Christ has welcomed you, for the glory of God.

Gentiles: For I tell you that Christ became a servant to the circumcised to show God's truthfulness, in order to confirm the promises given to the patriarchs,

Jews: And in order that the Gentiles might glorify God for God's mercy.

Gentiles: As it is written,

Jews: Therefore I will confess you among the Gentiles, and sing to your name (Ps. 18:49).

Gentiles: And again it is said,

Jews: Rejoice, O Gentiles, with his people;
and let all the peoples praise him (Deut. 32:43).

Leader: And further Isaiah says,

Gentiles: The root of Jesse shall come,
the one who rises to rule the Gentiles;
in him shall the Gentiles hope (Isa. 11:10).

All: May the God of hope fill you with all joy and peace in believing, so that by the power of the Holy Spirit you may abound in hope. Amen.

Debriefing and Applying

If there is discussion time after the meal, use it to reflect on any new insights from participating in the agape meal. Was it hard to stay in character and to sustain tensions around food when contemporary issues about food in our culture are so different? What questions might food arouse for us today? Guilt for overeating? Questions on the morality of drinking alcoholic beverages or of eating unhealthy foods? Boycotting foods like table grapes, Folger's coffee, Nestle's chocolate, or Coca Cola — because the companies that produce them are oppressive to powerless people? Guilt for throwing away food when starvation stalks so many people around the world?

These are North American issues. Once I led a simulation on Romans 14 with a group that included a number of international students. During our debriefing time, someone mentioned how different are our issues on food today than they were in the Roman Empire of Paul's day. A man from Kenya disagreed. He said the problem of whether or not to eat meat offered to idols is a contemporary one in his culture. Often goats are sacrificed to appease the gods or evil spirits, and the rest of the meat is sold and eaten. Christians in his home community would argue heatedly over whether it was right to eat such meat. It was a strong point of contention.

On the practical level of living, Christian qualities of love and acceptance toward those with whom we disagree often fall by the wayside. What issues in your family, congregation, denomination, or religious organization have caused bitter feelings, resentments, and perhaps even splits? Could a firm belief in one's own convictions and true acceptance of others with different convictions heal the wounds? How can you apply the gospel's message of reconciliation in Paul's Roman letter to your situation today?

18 | Epilogue

Did Paul's letter make a difference to the house churches in Rome? Did he influence the Christian believers to work together in unity in the midst of their diversity? When did the gospel reach Spain? Much is in the dark.

We do know that Paul's hopes for evangelizing Spain were shattered by his arrest in Jerusalem while taking the collection back to the saints there (Acts 21–23; 24:17). He finally did reach Rome, but as a prisoner he remained under house arrest for two years (Acts 28:16-30). There is no mention of the house-church groups he had addressed several years earlier. Luke speaks of Paul preaching to the Jews. Some were convinced and others were not. Later tradition tells us that Paul was beheaded in Rome.

What of the fractured and contentious house churches? Peter Lampe comments, "In the later history of the Roman Church, this divided nature helped 'heresies' to survive in the capital city for decades. It also prevented the institution of a Roman monarchical bishop until the second half of the second century."[1] But when Paul wrote, some of that history was still far in the future, and we do not know his immediate impact. Some Christians recognized the value of Paul's letter. It was saved, treasured, and copied, to be read to other Christians around the Roman Empire and down to the present. It became part of the authoritative canon and thus a great gift to the whole church, not only to Rome and Spain, as Paul had earlier conceived.

Yet Paul's message of reconciliation of disparate people through Jesus Christ was often misinterpreted to further divide them. It is left to us to take up Phoebe's mission properly to proclaim and interpret Romans — and then put its message of unity in diversity into practice.

1. Lampe, "The Roman Christians," in *The Romans Debate*, 230.

I like to think, though, that Paul's letter and Phoebe's journey to Rome made an impact on many believers there. After I led this simulation of Romans with a seminary class, I asked each member to write reflections. Here is a letter written by Ann Moyer,[2] who played the role of Aurelia, a slave in the household of Prisca and Aquila. Aurelia writes to Phoebe shortly after she has visited them.

Household of Prisca and Aquila
The Aventine, Rome
May 15, 57

Dear Phoebe,

It was so exciting for me and all the members of our household to get to know you while you were with us last month. We often speak about the wonderful discussions we had with you about Paul's letter. It has meant much to us that Paul wrote such a thorough exposition of his understanding of God's plan for the Jews and how we Gentiles can now be reconciled to God through Jesus Christ our Lord — especially in light of our difficult circumstances here in Rome. Thank you for coming, not just to deliver Paul's letter but to explain and clarify what he had to say. I admire your leadership qualities greatly. I find myself thinking of you as a role model for myself as I explore what it means to be a woman in the church. Many thanks for the gift of yourself to us here in Rome.

Thinking back on those discussions, I remember many feelings of smugness I had as you read Paul's words to the Jews. So often those feelings were rapidly replaced by sheepishness when the next words were addressed to us Gentiles. Paul had a way of leveling people, which we desperately need. You learned what tensions there are between those who stayed on in Rome after Claudius's edict, and the Jews who are now returning to our churches.

Paul seemed to have a good grasp of the situation, too. I hope we all can take his advice and learn not to pass judgment or look down on

2. Used by permission of Ann Moyer, San Diego, California.

those whose practices are different from our own. I admit I've had problems with Brother Epaenetus's practices in the past. Sometimes he just seems so prudish, so bound by the law he has always kept!

But I must also tell you that he and I are not arguing as much about these things. Now there is less sniping at each other in our household than before we got Paul's letter. As I quit looking down on him for his weakness in this regard, I find that I appreciate his gentle spirit and kindness. I know he is sincere in his practice of the law.

Through our discussion, I came to a better understanding of my own sin. If we think we have no sin, we're really in trouble. When I was first converted, I felt that all my sin had rolled away. But when I am honest with myself, I become aware of more and more ways in which I do what Paul accused us of doing — things like exchanging the truth about God for a lie, wanting to control my own life, and not wanting to recognize the lordship of God in concrete ways. It's all wonderful to talk about, but Paul really pushes us to apply it to our own lives, offering our own "bodies as living sacrifices." Wow! I have so much to learn.

All the teaching was great! For me the high point of all our discussions came when Aquila told us that he and Prisca had decided to free all the slaves in the household. Words cannot express my joy (mixed with fear) at being a free woman for the first time. It gives me a whole new outlook on life! My creativity seems to be opening up by this change in circumstances, and I am producing wool pieces so different from those of the slave Aurelia. (I am always going to keep some of my old work, though, as a reminder of who I was — and I think there is great beauty in those pieces woven in my pain.) But it's exciting to just sit and *feel free!* Not that I get a whole lot of time to sit, even now. I have lots to do keeping up with all the awnings Aquila is turning out. Business is booming.

Prisca and Aquila send greetings. They are busy arranging for the house-church leaders to meet together to make some plans for follow-up study of Paul's letter. They hope this leadership group will be led by the Spirit to work at the issues raised in all the house churches, and between groups as well.

Epaenetus says to give you his greetings. He is excited by Paul's words about the Holy Spirit and may be writing to you soon about his ideas. Soullios is Soullios. He's been making frequent buying trips as usual, and I pray that he will be strong and resist those traps of the world which he encounters so frequently. Doria is a joy to us all — and sends her love. She also looks up to you a great deal.

We haven't seen Felicia since she moved to the household of Robertson.[3] I was surprised at her sudden leaving, but she'll be happier where they all think more alike. She certainly doesn't like conflict, although she knows how to argue well. We often pray for her happiness.

Thank you again, Phoebe, for your sojourn with us. We needed the letter from Paul, as well as the understanding you brought along with it. Paul sure can be tough to understand sometimes. We all enjoyed our last day with you so much — the food and fellowship were a real blessing. I felt like we were living what we'd just heard from Paul. And we've been doing more of that ever since.

I hope this finds you well and that the journey back to Cenchreae was not too difficult. When you see Paul again, let him know how much we appreciated the letter. Here in Rome, we have great enthusiasm for his mission to Spain. That is one thing everyone seems to agree on: the gospel must be carried to the ends of the earth.

God's blessing until we meet again,

Your sister,
Aurelia

3. This refers to a class member from a fundamentalist church who dropped out of class apparently because she couldn't handle the diverse opinions. She already had been making plans to attend Pat Robertson's Regent University Divinity School.

APPENDIX 1 | Leader's Guide

Who Can Use This Book?

This book invites the individual reader, yet best results will be gained if the simulation technique mentioned throughout is used with a group of people. Group learning through simulation will bring out a wealth of truths and nuances that cannot otherwise be gained.

Both the writing style and the content are meant to include as wide a range of learners as possible: upper high school age to adults in church school or other Christian education classes; and high school, college, or seminary students in a regular academic program. Material can also be adapted to settings at a conference or camp.

This text, used with the Bible, is adequate for courses in church school and high school. For college and seminary classes, additional commentaries and other points of view are recommended. (See the end of this Guide.)

Who Should Lead the Simulation?

The best leader for this simulation is not necessarily a "teacher" — in the sense of someone who knows a lot of information and can lecture well to a group of students. Instead, the class will need an organizer, someone who can set the stage for learning and guide group discussions. The leader must be prepared for learning which is not always systematic but is highly participatory. Students who participate in their own learning retain it better than when they only listen to lectures. An attitude of creativity, innovation, and risk-taking will be an asset.

Yet each lesson is carefully structured. Results will be successful only if the leader maintains control and makes sure each member understands the material and fully participates in a role. Once the class is ready to begin the simulation, the structure for each lesson remains the same.

Preparing to Lead the Romans Simulation

Some of the suggestions below will be more applicable to a church congregation than an academic setting.

Publicity

This method of Bible study may not be familiar to many people. Since it demands a specific time commitment, you may need to publicize it weeks ahead of time. If your church has a weekly bulletin, you can use notices to tease and attract participants weeks before the class begins.

Time Commitment

Regular attendance in the course is a must for two reasons: (1) Each person role-plays a particular character in a particular house church and is necessary to the total functioning of that group. (2) The experience in each session builds on the previous session.

A Sunday school setting may be the most difficult for expecting regular attendance. For these situations it may be best for the leader to have in hand copies of the "Visitor's Guide to Rome" (a following appendix) and extra character sketches (derived from chapter 6) written on slips of paper to hand to visitors.

The ideal time limit is 12 or 13 sessions of two hours each. However, this is adjustable. Since the simulation does not actually begin until chapter 8, chapters 1–7 can be read outside class. The first two class periods, then, can be used for clarifying questions, organizing house-church groups, and developing characters.

Once the simulation begins, best results will be gained by a continuous one- to two-hour block of time. In high school class periods limited to 45 minutes or so, the simulation can be done in one period, with the follow-up discussion held in the next. Given a choice, however, a two-period block is preferable to two separate periods.

My most successful experience leading this course was during a seminary January term. The class met each morning for at least two hours, with a short break halfway through. Twice a week we met for additional sessions to discuss other scholarly perspectives on Romans.

Size of Class

If possible, find out ahead of time the approximate number of participants. In order for *all* house churches mentioned in Romans 16 to function, you will need a minimum of 28-30 participants besides the leader, and a maximum of 50. This will allow for at least five or six people in each group and no more than ten, including the returning Jewish refugees who would like to be received back.

For 23 to 27 participants, eliminate "the household of Narcissus" and work with four house churches. For 18 to 22, eliminate both "Narcissus" and "the Saints." For 12 to 17, divide them between the house church of Prisca and Aquila and the "Brothers and Sisters." One member in each group (or two if the group has more than 6) should be a Jewish exile returning home.

In a group of 11 or less, all should be members of Prisca's and Aquila's house church. Have a cross-section of a household containing slave and free, richer and poorer, Jew and Gentile, conservative and liberal.

Shared Leadership

If you know persons in your class, you may want to choose house-church leaders ahead of time to make sure there is one person in each group who feels comfortable guiding a discussion. They may prefer to read the first six or seven chapters of this book ahead of time and choose which house church they would like to lead.

The house church of Prisca and Aquila should be co-led by this couple, probably with Prisca as main leader. For the "Brothers and Sisters" and the "Saints," the designated leader should choose an appropriate name mentioned in Romans 16. A man will therefore have to lead the "Brothers and Sisters"; either sex can lead the "Saints." Choices are entirely open for the other two house churches.

Phoebe or Her Secretary

Essential for the simulation is a woman to play the role of Phoebe — or a man or woman to be her secretary. This role can be filled by the leader-teacher or one of the students who will be playing another role during the rest of the simulation. Choose someone with a good reading voice. Phoebe may be of such a high class that she would not read the text herself but would leave this task to her secretary, who would have skills as a professional rhetor. (In the original situation, Phoebe herself would have interpreted and expanded on Paul's letter.) For our purposes, it seems least complicated to have a woman playing the role of Phoebe and reading the text. This is a way of communicating the importance of women leaders in Paul's mission of proclaiming the gospel.

Materials

- A copy of this text for each participant
- A Bible for each participant
- Pencils or pens
- Reusable name tags (plastic with paper insert)
- Poster board (or foam board or manila folders) and felt-tip markers for sign and logo identifying each house church
- Refreshments. These are optional and may depend on the time the class meets. Use foods eaten in the Middle East — grape juice, wheat crackers, raisins, nuts, or dates.

A Note about Signs

These are primarily a creative, right-brain activity used to identify groups and provide some *esprit de corps*. When preparing to teach this class in Sunday school at my congregation, I bought one large piece of foam board and cut it into six pieces, each about 12 by 16 inches. A woodworker in our group made stands for the signs. He drilled holes in small flat pieces of plywood, glued sturdy 3-foot dowels into them, and attached signs to the top of the dowels with hot wax. The groups drew their logos on the other side.

However, one could simply prop signs on a chair or hang them from the wall during each class period.

Background Sessions: Reconstructing Rome and the Christian House Churches

The first seven chapters of this book contain necessary information for establishing house churches and developing characters in these cell groups. The number and length of sessions the leader allows for this preparation depends on time constraints and the maturity, advance knowledge, and preparation of participants. To prepare members for roles, use at least two sessions of an hour or more, preferably three sessions. I recommend the following:

> Session One: chapters 1–2 in this book
> Session Two: chapters 3–4
> Session Three: chapters 5–7

Session One

Objectives

1. To introduce the method of simulation as a tool for understanding Paul's letter to the Roman Christians.

2. To understand the geography of the Roman Empire, why Paul wanted to write to the Romans, and how this desire related to his plan to take the gospel to Spain.
3. To understand the history of the Jews in Rome and how this history relates to Paul's letter to the Romans.

Preliminary Discussion

Time will be saved if participants can obtain the book and read the first two chapters before the first session. If adults have read the first two chapters, discuss these issues:

1. How does this sociohistorical simulation approach differ from other ways you have learned about Romans (or other biblical writings)? Are some methods of interpreting the Bible more valid or more appropriate than others?
2. How do you feel about the simulation technique?
3. Discuss questions in chapter 2 about Paul, his interests in visiting Rome, and the Spanish mission.
4. Review history of the Jews in Rome and its importance for understanding Paul's letter.

Some classes have limited knowledge of Romans and will not have read this book ahead of time. Ask the class what they already know about Romans. (Some may know nothing beyond a vague thought that Paul wrote it.) Further questions: Did Paul write this letter before or after visiting the Roman Christians? Did Paul found this church as he did the churches in Corinth, Thessalonica, and Philippi? Was there only one church in Rome? How familiar are you with key texts such as 1:16-17; 8:28, 31-39; 10:9-10?

Orientation

1. Explain the simulation process and how Romans 16 gives clues to house churches and individual characters.
2. Look at map of Roman Empire to see where Paul had traveled thus far and why Rome was strategic for his plans.
3. Read Romans 15:15-29 together and discuss questions at the beginning of chapter 2, about Paul and the Spanish mission.
4. Go over history of Jews in Rome, preferably writing out a time line on a chalkboard or newsprint.

With a high school class, especially in a church school or camp situation, it may be best to explain the simulation technique immediately, show them Romans 16, and ask them to find five groupings in that chapter. Then talk about how each of them will be role-playing a character in one of these church groups. Stress the variety of emphases they will be choosing from — conservative or liberal, Jew or Gentile, rich or poor, slave, freedperson, or freeperson.

A possible technique for drawing in kids immediately may be to photocopy the descriptions of house churches and characters found in chapter 6, cut them apart, divide up the group immediately, and give each person a copy of the description of the group they are in. Hand out name tags, and they can choose their name and other strategic information immediately. Have them write it down on the character sketch in chapter 3.

Then move to items 2-4 in the above list. It may seem like working backwards, but having already chosen a character may motivate kids toward learning the reason *why* their character belongs to a particular household, why there is tension and rivalry among the Christians in Rome, and why they might be interested in Paul's letter.

Assign chapters 3–4 for next session.

Session Two

Objectives

1. To establish house-church groups and individual characters in each group.
2. To develop individual characters through information given in chapters 3–4.
3. To introduce each church and individual in it to the other groups.
4. To create signs with names and logos advertising their house church.

Forming Groups

In this session, the leader will help the group divide into smaller house churches (if there are more than 10 participants and this has not already been done). Give everyone a name tag and have them begin filling out the character sketch in chapter 3. If the members flounder, they may read in chapter 6 the imaginative reconstructions of personalities in their own house church. This will help with name, occupation, status, and racial origin, and it will show how they fit together as a house church.

If you have chosen *small-group leaders* ahead of time, they can help work out a good balance in their group. Making sure there are persons of each variety in each group is essential to the richness of discussion that will follow once the simulation has begun. Pronounced personality types or caricatures (such as superconservative or superliberal) will increase the spice and humor. However, do not press members to have a fully developed character at this point. Many nuances are still to come.

Hand out scratch paper, poster board, and markers. Each group should create a name and logo appropriate for their house church. *Collect all name tags, signs, and markers at the close of the session.*

Assign chapters 5–7 for next session.

Session Three

Objectives

1. To further develop characters and house churches by integrating religious backgrounds into the character sketches.
2. To discuss rhetorical styles and the rhetorical outline of Romans.

Learning Activities

Hand out name tags and signs. Allow time at the beginning for questions about Roman religions from chapter 5. Give the class time to work in house-church groups to further fill out character sketches with information from chapter 5. If there is more than one group, each should also develop an overall "character" for their house church, as described in chapter 3.

Then have a spokesperson from each group *introduce the group* to all the others by showing the sign and calling each member by her or his "Roman" name. Have members share with each other about their former religions and how they were converted. Testimony time!

Devote the second half of this session to *discussing chapter 7*, the rhetorical structure of Romans. Though this may seem boring to some, it is essential to understand Romans as a *speech* and have a grasp of its outline. Understanding the literary *structure* of Romans is necessary for understanding its *content* and main idea.

1. Ask the class for examples of particular styles or structure used in literature or the media today (such as small sound bytes when reporting news on TV; heavily illustrated children's books; cheap and accessible paperback format for popular novels and how-to books; extreme realism of illustrations in fantasy novels; the persuasive, manipulative, superconfident air of many televangelists, and so on).
2. Ask the class to evaluate speeches, such as political speeches at the Democratic or Republican conventions during a presidential campaign, speeches in assemblies at their school, or sermons in church.

How is structure and style used to persuade listeners? Have they ever heard an ambassador's speech? How are these speeches structured to emphasize good will between nations?

3. Have the class look at Paul's introduction to his letter to the Romans (1:1-15) and compare its length with his introductions in 1 Corinthians, Galatians, and Philippians. *Why is the Romans intro so much longer?* (Paul wants to appeal directly to each ethnic group in the Roman churches and deal with tensions that exist among them. He uses vocabulary and specific phrases that will include everyone.) Stress the politico-theological agenda — persuading Jews and Gentiles to get along together in unity — in Paul's speech and his use of ancient Greco-Roman rhetorical principles to convey that agenda.

4. Write an outline of Romans on chalkboard. Use it to show how the speech will be studied throughout the course — and how each proof leads back to the thesis statement in Romans 1:16-17.

5. Close with an enthusiastic reminder that the simulation itself will begin with the following session. All the work done on character development and understanding first-century Rome will immediately be put to use from then on to the end of the course.

For next session, assign Romans 1:1-17; 15:14–16:23; and chapter 8 of this book. Reading the necessary material beforehand is a must for successful simulation.

Session Four

Objectives

1. To introduce "Phoebe" or her secretary as the proclaimer of Romans.
2. To begin actual simulation of the Roman house churches.
3. To examine the introduction and conclusion of Romans and establish its purpose, parameters, and mood.
4. To connect Paul's theology of inclusiveness with our theology and actions in this arena today.

Structure of Session Four and Later Sessions

- Getting in gear — 15 min.
- Phoebe's introduction and reading — 20 min.
- House-church discussions — 30 min.
- Debriefing and applying — 30 min.
- Refreshments? — 15 min.

Getting in Gear

Arrange for signs, name tags, pencils, this textbook, a Bible for each participant, and refreshments if desired. Members sit in area of their small
group. Stress that everyone must assume their role throughout Phoebe's
introduction, the reading of the text, and house-church discussion. Only
during debriefing may they move into the present and discuss and analyze
the simulation, their own roles, and the interpretation of the text for today.
At the end of Phoebe's introduction, members of the class may greet her
individually with a hug; a kiss on each cheek, Middle Eastern style; or a
handshake. Applause may be substituted.

Reassure the class that the character each is playing is important to
the discussion, no matter how outrageous their character's opinions. Extreme opinions *should* be put forth, so that as the study proceeds, some
might be tempered by hearing Paul's arguments. To the original audience,
Paul's letter was not authoritative Scripture. Though he was well-known
and had a powerful personality, his primary authority lay over the churches
he himself had founded. The Roman churches were not among them; hence
his attempt to be diplomatic and persuasive, rather than commanding.

Phoebe's Introduction and Reading

Prisca or Aquila (or whoever is assigned) introduces Phoebe (see chapter
8). After personal greetings, Phoebe acknowledges the introduction and
proceeds to read Romans 1:1-17 and 15:14–16:27.

House-Church Discussions

Use questions near the end of chapter 8. Small-group leaders should make sure discussion moves forward and should attempt to include everyone. If the class is so small that only the house church of Prisca and Aquila is represented, Prisca should lead that group, but the class leader-teacher can participate, perhaps playing the role of Phoebe or of someone from another house church.

When I led this course with only one house church, I made different signs saying PHOEBE and names of one member of each of the other groups. When the group seemed to need further elucidation of Paul's letter, I held up the PHOEBE sign and interpreted Paul as Phoebe no doubt did herself. When the group seemed to need an extra perspective that wasn't represented in the group, or when they needed to be reminded of a rival house church in their city, I changed signs and played a different role to jar them a bit or shift the conversation.

If there is more than one group, the leader can play the role of Phoebe throughout the discussion and move from one group to another to clarify or interpret.

Debriefing and Applying

Unless the group is unusually large, it is best to handle this discussion with the entire class. After a 20- or 30-minute first-century discussion period, call out, "Cut!" or whatever ritual the leader uses to bring the groups back through the time machine to the present. Then use the questions at the end of chapter 8 to guide the debriefing and application discussion.

For this first session, probably more time will be spent analyzing the simulation, since it is a new experience. However, as people get used to role-playing, later sessions should move quickly into reflection on how to apply Paul's message to our contemporary situations. That, after all, is the primary purpose for studying Romans. Applications are not always easy to make; it will be the leader's job to continually stress this connection.

Assign Romans 1:18–3:31 and chapter 9 of this book for the next session. If this class meets for a full two hours, especially if in the evening, you may want to serve simple refreshments of Middle Eastern foods (see chapter 17).

Sessions Five through Twelve

The structure of all of these sessions will be similar to Session Four, minus Phoebe's introduction. Use a few minutes to get organized and make sure all participants have the proper materials and know the roles they are playing. Take time to answer questions of clarification about chapter 9 in the text or about Romans 1:18–3:31 that cannot be dealt with during the simulation.

At this stage in each session, *call attention to the outline* of Romans and show how the section under consideration fits into the outline and into the total thrust of the letter. Periodically remind students that the letter was meant to be read as an entire speech, with each section integrally tied to those before and after. At the beginning of each session, give a brief review of what has gone before.

Then proceed to the *simulation,* with Phoebe reading the text, followed by house-church discussion. Cut off simulation to allow time at the end of the period to *debrief* and discuss contemporary *applications* of Paul's message (finish in the next period if time runs short).

Assign the appropriate chapter to read by next class period.

Session Thirteen

Most of the plans for this session — the agape meal — are included in the text of this book, chapter 17.

Preparation

The leader will need to arrange for an adequate room for the meal and a table or two for food. If space is cramped and people must sit on the floor, it will be like first-century agape meals. Bowls and cups made of fired clay are more authentic, but you may settle for paperware. Forks were not yet invented, so bring only spoons and several sharp communal knives. Napkins were likely not in use at the time, but most of us don't like to do without. Bring an uncut loaf of bread, grape juice (or diluted wine), and a goblet or cup for Eucharist.

The agape meal can be eaten by separate house-church groups. But it will be more fun to have everyone celebrate together, like a conference-wide, diocese-wide, or citywide gathering today. Visitors may be attending, so provide extra name tags (one-time stickers are okay) and a list of extra names from which visitors can choose.

Structure of Session

1. As participants come (wearing their name tags), they can set their food on the table and mingle with others. Ask one or two persons to be responsible for arranging food (perhaps those role-playing waiters or cooks).

2. When all have gathered, remind participants to experience this meal in character, expressing their first-century personality, as they have in the small groups. When mingling with members from other groups, they will get to know those characters. Ask about their lives in various households, their work for a living, their thoughts about Paul's letter. . . . If class members bring visitors, encourage members to choose a Roman name from your list for their visitors and help the visitors create characters for themselves. Visitors may be someone met at the marketplace; a client or benefactor; or visiting relatives from Egypt, Macedonia, or another province.

3. Celebrate communion, eat the agape meal, repeat closing litany, and handle the post-meal discussion time as described in chapter 17.

Session Fourteen (optional)

If there is time for an extra session (with no simulation), this could provide a time of closure for the group.

Objectives

1. To draw overall conclusions about the relevance of Romans to the Christian life today.
2. To discuss interpretive issues that have not been adequately addressed earlier in the course.
3. To discuss various methods of biblical interpretation, such as those listed in the next appendix.
4. To evaluate the method and content of the course.

Suggested Structure of Session

1. *Welcome* group together for the last time. See that everyone has a Bible and a copy of this text. Since the structure is different, go over objectives with the class.
2. *Interpretation* Have group read and discuss the next appendix on varied "Models of Interpretation." Make sure everyone understands the word *hermeneutics* and the four models. The class can see that there is not one simple way of interpreting the Bible, that texts are not as plain and obvious as some lead us to believe, and that one comes to different conclusions depending on the model one uses.

   Stress, however, that these models are not necessarily exclusive of each other. Aspects of all four can be used. Ask: Which model have we used most heavily in this course? (pastoral-theological). In what ways have we used all four models? (The doctrinal model was used to search for timeless truths; the historical-critical for information in setting up house churches; the pastoral-theological for the interaction during the simulation and debriefing; and the liberation model for gaining insight into issues of race, wealth and poverty, and gender issues.)

3. Discuss *theological issues* raised throughout this course on Romans. You may want to bring up questions not adequately dealt with earlier for lack of time, or those that particularly struck a nerve or provoked a range of opinions. Or ponder questions from the appendix on "Contemporary Issues."

Less academic and more personal approaches:

a. What did the character you role-played teach you? What could you see through the eyes of that character that you might have missed otherwise?

b. Pressing further, you might say: In this course we have learned that God's grace is free to anyone and cannot be earned by keeping the law, by being born with any special pedigree, or by any good works by which we might try to win brownie points. Yet the life lived in faithful response to that grace is a life of holiness and obedience. There is an interesting phrase in the opening of Paul's speech in 1:4-5, where he talks about "Jesus Christ our Lord, through whom we have received grace and apostleship to *bring about the obedience of faith* among all the Gentiles for the sake of his name." Paul uses the same phrase to end his speech. In the closing benediction of 16:25-27, he commends the Roman Christians to "God who is able to strengthen you according to . . . the proclamation of Jesus Christ . . . *to bring about the obedience of faith.*"

In this course, what have we learned about "the obedience of faith"? If the mood allows, use this time as a sharing period, where members have a chance to articulate spiritual truths they may have gained during the course, or to share juicy tidbits from the small-group discussions.

This session may be ended by the group holding hands in a circle and the leader offering the benediction of Romans 16:25-27.

Teaching Variations and Adaptations

What if you cannot arrange for thirteen sessions? It is best to begin by leaving out the most familiar, most abstract parts, such as Romans 5–8.

Keep material more directly and concretely related to first-century Roman Christians.

Alternate Patterns

- *Ten sessions:* Use three to get organized, one each for Romans 1:1-17 and 15–16; 1–3; 7 or 8 (or 7–8 combined); 9–11; 12–13; 14; agape meal.
- *Eight sessions:* Omit Romans 5–8 and agape meal.
- *Six sessions:* Use two to get organized, but everyone reads chapters 1–7 in this book. Use chapters on Romans 1–3, including Paul's thesis in 1:16-17; 9–11; 12–13; 14.
- *Four sessions:* Participants read chapters 1–7 in this book. Use a session to get organized (map; history of Jews in Rome; establish house churches; assign character roles). Use chapters on Romans 1–3 including thesis in 1:16-17; 9–11; 14. If five sessions, add on Romans 12–13.
- *One session:* Hand out slips giving character sketches from chapter 6. Explain reasons for tension within and among house churches and use only Romans 14.

For College or Seminary Courses

The house-church discussions should be enriched by assigned readings in other sources. I recommend two essential commentaries:

Both college and seminary students will benefit from Robert Jewett's *Romans,* Cokesbury Basic Bible Commentary (Nashville: Graded Press, 1988), which my book follows in its outline of Paul's letter. Since my simulation was developed through study with Robert Jewett, this small lay commentary provides additional insight into how Paul's original audience would have understood his letter.[1]

A scholarly commentary which takes Paul's original audience and

---

1. See also Robert Jewett, *Romans,* Hermeneia (Minneapolis: Fortress, 2006).

political and social issues into account is James D. G. Dunn's *Word Biblical Commentary*, vol. 38A: *Romans 1–8*; and vol. 38B: *Romans 9–16* (Waco: Word Books, 1988). When I taught this course in seminary, Dunn was required reading. Dunn includes a comprehensive bibliography and dialogues with many other scholars.

A third possible text is *Paul's Gospel in an Intercultural Context* by William S. Campbell (New York: Peter Lang, 1991). This collection of essays on various parts of Romans shows how sociology impacts theology in Paul's letter.

In college or seminary classes, extra sessions should be held where Romans can be seen from other perspectives. Most helpful to me has been *The Romans Debate*, edited by Karl P. Donfried, revised and expanded (Peabody, Mass.: Hendrickson, 1991). In these essays, Donfried brings together major Romans scholars from various twentieth-century time periods and perspectives. It is instructive to see how they disagree with each other!

Students should also be regularly reading another commentary besides Dunn in order to compare viewpoints, which can then be shared in class. I recommend Martin Luther, along with other traditional texts from Lutheran or Reformed perspectives (Nygren, Murray, etc.).

Students who want further to explore the sociological and historical background of Romans will find many resources in the bibliography near the end of this book.

APPENDIX 2 | Models of Biblical Interpretation

"Hermeneutics" is a long word with a simple meaning. It refers to interpretation, usually in reference to the Bible. But the task of interpreting the Bible is far from simple. When we are dealing with writings from ancient cultures so different from ours, we often don't understand them and give up trying. Or we misinterpret them, which sometimes can have negative or disastrous consequences.

Below are simplified descriptions of four methods of biblical interpretation.[1] Which model is most familiar to you? Which method or combination of methods do you find most helpful? Which model or models have we depended on most heavily in this study of Romans?

Doctrinal Model

This perspective sees the Bible as the divine Word of God, with timeless truths clearly set forth for people in any age and culture. In its most conservative form, this model insists on verbal inspiration and inerrancy. It provides proof texts for the doctrines it holds. Much energy is used to harmonize the various documents and apparent contradictions in the Bible.

Another form of the doctrinal model is the liturgical, which uses texts (such as lectionary readings) for worship and expects them to be meaningful even when not placed in literary and historical context.

1. Fuller discussions can be found in two books by Elisabeth Schüssler Fiorenza: *Bread Not Stone: The Challenge of Feminist Biblical Interpretation* (Boston: Beacon, 1984), 25-42; and *In Memory of Her: A Feminist Theological Reconstruction of Christian Origins* (New York: Crossroad, 1983), 4-6.

Historical-critical Model

This approach sees the Bible as an artifact of the past, and of human origin. It emphasizes scientific observation and tries to unearth historical facts behind the biblical writings. It can accept as true only what can be proved to have "actually happened." It insists on neutral objectivity in the search for accuracy.

Pastoral-theological Model

This method sees the biblical writings as pastoral and theological treatises used in the various communities of faith out of which they emerged. Such a perspective helps explain differences in the Gospels and why Paul said different things to different churches.

The model uses historical criticism, but it also reflects on the interaction between the text and its original audience, and between the text and its listeners today. It is less invested in harmonizing Scripture (as in the doctrinal model). Diversity in the canon reflects many different faith communities which produced writings now in our Bible.

Liberation Model

This approach criticizes the other three for not admitting their political investments. Nobody can be objective, say the liberation theologians. All our opinions are skewed by our own frame of reference. The biblical texts are not objective. They show that God has a definite bias in favor of the poor and oppressed. Therefore, it is the underdogs to whom the Bible is really directed. Only with such an advocacy approach can biblical truth really be grasped.

A small book that offers further help in hermeneutics is Perry B. Yoder's *Toward Understanding the Bible: Hermeneutics for Lay People*.[2]

2. Perry B. Yoder, *Toward Understanding the Bible: Hermeneutics for Lay People* (Newton, Kans.: Faith & Life Press, 1978).

APPENDIX 3 | Aids to Conducting a Simulation of
Roman House-Church Dynamics

Creating Individual Characters for Role Play

Questions to Ask Yourself

- What is your name and your house church? Are you a slave, a freedperson, or freeborn?
- What is your occupation? How many hours a day do you work? Where do you work? With whom?
- Where do you live? What are your living quarters like? With whom do you live? Do they also attend your house church?
- How important to you is your participation in your house church?
- Are you educated? Intelligent? (Uneducated persons may be intelligent, and vice-versa!)

If you are Jewish:

- Did you leave Rome because of Claudius' edict? Or were you a slave, or too poor, or did you pretend to be a Gentile? If you left Rome in A.D. 49, how did you fare economically or socially?
- Why did you join a Christian house church? Because you disliked all the rules and regulations in Judaism? Because all your friends and family joined? Because you think the Christians understand Judaism correctly?
- Do you still participate in a Jewish synagogue in Rome?
- Do you have family or friends in Palestine?

If you are Gentile:

- Why did you join the Christian house church? Because you were attracted to Judaism and this group of Jewish folks accepted uncircumcised Gentiles? Because you were attracted to the stories of their leader Jesus? Because you think the Christian philosophy is better than other philosophies? Because it gave you a group to belong to, and your friends also joined? Because you were attracted to Jewish law and a high standard of ethics?
- What were your religious beliefs before joining the Christian house church? How have they changed?
- Do you still participate in other religions in Rome?

Inductive Preparation for Role-Playing House Churches
Hearing Romans 1:1-17 and 15:14–16:23

Before class, read chapter 8 in Finger's book and Romans 1:1-17 and 15:14–16:23. Then follow these directions and answer these questions.

1. The salutation and greetings in 1:1-7 are longer than in any other letter of Paul's. Underline any words or phrases that you think would especially appeal to the Jewish members of the Roman house churches. CIRCLE the words or phrases that would especially appeal to the non-Jews. Draw a WAVY LINE under the words Paul uses to describe himself.
2. In 1:8-15, underline why Paul thanks God for the Roman Christians. Underline any reasons Paul gives for why he wants to visit these churches in Rome. Is Paul acting authoritatively or diplomatically in this paragraph?
3. CIRCLE the thesis statement in Romans 1 for Paul's entire argument (see chapter 7 in this book).
4. Underline "the obedience of faith" in 1:5 and 16:26. Is this a contradiction in terms?
5. In 15:14-21, underline phrases or sentences that show that Paul thinks

he is especially commissioned to proclaim the gospel to non-Jews. Underline the part that tells you that Paul is NOT coming to Rome to preach the gospel there.

6. In 15:22-29, underline the reason why Paul cannot come to Rome now and the reason he wants to come later. Draw a WAVY LINE under the part that shows Paul is worried about his trip to Jerusalem.

7. In 16:1-16, underline the references to five house churches or cell groups. Star the one you are in. CIRCLE the names of people who are especially commended by Paul.

8. In 16:17-27, CIRCLE the names of people in Corinth who are sending their greetings to the Roman believers.

Inductive Preparation for Role-Playing House Churches Hearing Romans 1:18–3:31

1. Underline and draw a line between the phrase "the righteousness of God is revealed" in 1:17 with its opposite parallel in 1:18.

2. In 18-23, underline how God's power and divinity have been seen and understood by people. Underline what happened to them when they did not honor or thank God. Underline how such people became idolaters.

3. In 24-27, are the sexual immoralities described the *cause* or the *result* of idolatry? Underline the recurring phrase (also in v. 28) that clarifies this. In this description of immoral sex, underline all the words that relate to *lust* rather than *committed love*.

4. In 28-32, underline 18 or 19 other sins Paul identifies. Are vv. 18-32 more descriptive of the sins of Gentiles or Jews?

5. In 2:1-12, Paul is imagining speaking to a Jewish person who has just heard this long list of sins in chapter 1 and is condemning such people. Underline what Paul thinks of such a person.

6. In 2:1-16, CIRCLE the sentences that state what will happen to those who do good works and keep (the spirit of) the law.

7. In 2:17-34, underline the sins that are more typical of Jews. In 2:25-29, underline Paul's view of the meaning of circumcision.

8. In 3:1-7, CIRCLE the three imagined responses of Paul's imaginary Jewish dialogue partner to what he says in chapter 2. <u>Underline</u> Paul's retorts. (This kind of debate with an imaginary dialogue partner is called a *diatribe*, and Paul uses it often throughout Romans.)

9. In 3:9-18, how many Old Testament texts does Paul quote? From which book do most of them come?

10. In 3:21-26, CIRCLE the two parts of the OT that attest to God's righteousness for *all* who believe. Notice the **three** ways Paul describes how people can be rightwised. <u>Underline</u> the one that would appeal most to Jews. Draw a WAVY LINE under the one that would appeal most to slaves.

11. In 3:27-31, CIRCLE the reason boasting is excluded and the reason why God is also the God of Gentiles.

Inductive Preparation for Role-Playing House Churches
Hearing Romans 7:7–8:39

1. In 7:7-13, <u>underline</u> what Paul thinks about the Law. CIRCLE the word, used repeatedly, that Paul thinks is the real villain.

2. In 7:14-25, <u>underline</u> anything that you personally feel you can identify with in your own life, if anything.

3. Reread the two meanings of "flesh" on pp. 107-108. In 8:1-9, CIRCLE "flesh" whenever it means something negative. Put a BOX around it whenever it means simply "being human."

4. In 8:9-11, draw a WAVY LINE under Paul's reasoning for how believers receive eternal life.

5. In 8:9-17, <u>underline</u> all the things the Spirit of God does for the believer.

6. In 8:18-25, <u>underline</u> any information about the present condition and future hope of the created world we live in.

7. Explain the connection between the future of the creation (18-23) and bodily resurrection (11 and 23).

8. In 8:26-30, <u>underline</u> any insights of Paul's that are meaningful to you personally.

9. In 8:31-39, CIRCLE all the difficult things Christians may have to face in life. Underline any words or phrases of comfort and hope.

Inductive Preparation for Role-Playing House Churches Hearing Romans 9–11

1. In 9:1-5, underline Paul's attitude toward those Jews who do not yet believe in Jesus as Messiah. CIRCLE all the privileges and blessings which the Jews have had.
2. In 9:6, Paul says that not all Israelites truly belong to Israel. CIRCLE the names of three persons on whom God unexpectedly showed mercy, and draw a BOX around the name of one who did not receive mercy.
3. In 9:19-29, how many texts does Paul refer to from his scriptures (LXX, which includes the Apocrypha)? Which books are they from? Why do only two of your cross-references include "LXX"?
4. In 9:30–10:4, underline why Israel did not attain righteousness, and what it is that they do have, but not in the correct way (see pp. 117-118).
5. In 10:5-21, underline all the scripture quotations. How many are there, and from what sections of the Hebrew Bible do they come (that is, law, prophets, wisdom)?
6. In 11:1-10, underline v. 5 as a key verse and CIRCLE the word that represents the *believing* Jews. In the margin, write the names of the believing Jews in your house church, including yours, if you are a Jew.
7. In 11:11-12, underline where Paul explains why so few Jews have not yet come to believe.
8. CIRCLE the audience to whom Paul specifically speaks in 11:13-24. Underline the image he uses to describe these people. Underline the phrase that explains what keeps these people in their place.
9. In 11:25, underline anything that shows God has not given up on unbelieving Jews.

Inductive Preparation for Role-Playing House Churches
Hearing Romans 12–13

1. In 12:1-2, <u>underline</u> what every Jew or Gentile Christian is called to do in Rome instead of traveling to Jerusalem to do.
2. In 12:3-8, <u>underline</u> what Christians are supposed to think or not think. CIRCLE the gifts given for the one body. Is this a complete or a representative list? <u><u>Double underline</u></u> the gifts which are gender-specific.
3. <u>Underline</u> the exhortations in 12:9-13 that might be especially relevant to the precarious economic and social situation of the returning Jewish refugees.
4. Are the instructions in 12:14-21 directed mainly to Jews or Gentiles? See pp. 126-127 for reasons why. <u>Underline</u> any behaviors in this paragraph that Jesus modeled for his followers.
5. Read carefully the discussion on taxes and government in pp. 127-128. Then <u>underline</u> everything in 13:1-7 that you believe applies to Christians at all times and places and in every political situation, no matter what government one lives under. (Do not forget the war cry of the American Revolution: "No taxation without representation!")
6. In 13:8-10, <u>underline</u> any laws from the Old Testament that Paul believes are still relevant. <u>Underline</u> their references in the list of cross-references.
7. In 13:11-14, <u>underline</u> clues to how soon Paul expects the Lord Jesus to return. CIRCLE the more typical sins of Gentiles or liberals. Put a BOX around typical sins of Jews or conservatives.

Inductive Preparation for Role-Playing House Churches
Hearing Romans 14:1–15:6

1. In the introductory paragraph (14:1-4), <u>underline</u> the sentence that explains what the disagreement is about. In v. 3, CIRCLE the verbs that characterize how the two groups are relating to each other. What is the difference between these two verbs?

2. In the space before chapter 14, write your Roman name and whether you are "weak" (conservative) or "strong" (liberal).

3. In the second paragraph, underline the second issue the Roman Christians are arguing about. CIRCLE the sentence that shows Paul's amazing tolerance on this issue. Underline the repeated phrase in v. 6 that explains why Paul is so tolerant.

4. In the fourth paragraph (vv. 10-12), underline the sentence that explains why believers do not need to judge or despise each other.

5. In the fifth paragraph (vv. 13-23), three positions about food are represented: liberal, conservative, and wavering. CIRCLE references to these three positions. Underline all the imperative sentences where Paul directly tells his audience what to do or not to do. To which group is most advice directed?

6. In 15:1, the word "strong" is used for the first time. In Greek, it is *dunamis,* which means "powerful" (it's where we get our word "dynamite"). The word for "weak" is *a-dunamis,* or "without power." These terms now point more to political power or the lack of it in the house churches. The liberals seem to be in the majority. To which group is 15:1-6 directed? What does Paul expect them to do to make peace?

7. Which two Old Testament texts are referred to in 14:1–15:6? Underline them in your cross-references. Why does the Isaiah reference include an LXX? Look up the Maccabees references alluded to in 15:4. Why do you think these cross-references are included?

Sample Page from Romans "Diary"

(Student role-playing Aurelia, from the church in the house of Prisca and Aquila)

Dear Diary,

Today was an unusual day — a day I had been looking forward to all week. Ever since Phoebe of Cenchreae arrived, we had heard that one of the Christian missionaries, Paul of Tarsus, had written a letter just for the believers in Rome. Phoebe, of course, is Paul's co-worker and patron down near Corinth.

Well, today we finally heard the beginning of the letter — and Paul's greetings at the end. We could not get any farther because everyone wanted to talk about what Paul had said, even his opening lines! Our worship services are usually pretty lively, but this time *everybody* had something to say. Prisca, who led the meeting, could hardly get people to wait in line!

Some of our people think Paul is great because they met him back East and heard him preach. But Epaenetus is pretty wary. He is more conservative than Paul, and now he is afraid he is going to lose his battle with Felicia about eating only kosher meat. We have not heard yet if Paul said anything in his letter about keeping the food laws; maybe that is coming later. But Olympios is nervous about Paul's letter for the opposite reason. That old pagan thinks the whole Jewish law should be dumped! (I know I shouldn't call him "pagan," but I do it just to tease him.)

Well, I am just a slave, so I did not say much at first. But I heard Paul say that *he* was a slave, too — a slave of Jesus Christ. At first, I thought he was kidding. This guy is free to go wherever he wants; he is even a citizen of the Empire, just like my masters, Prisca and Aquila. But Aquila reminded me that Paul really does feel especially called by God to preach the gospel to the Gentiles, and he has been through more hardships than probably many slaves in this huge city.

So what did I think about Paul's opening greeting, after the "slave" part? I think he is trying really hard to get on our good side. He talked about Jesus "descended from David according to the flesh," so that made the Jews among us feel good. You know how they can lord it over the rest of us sometimes because they are the *real* Chosen People. But then right away Paul moved to our common belief in Jesus' resurrection from the dead, and how *that* is where Paul's power comes from, not so much that he was a Jew. Actually, I thought he was pretty inclusive, all things considered. I just wonder if he will be able to hold the attention of all the diverse people in our house church. Phoebe's visit sure will be exciting!

Practical Suggestions for Role-Playing House Churches Hearing Romans 13:1-7

For the house church of Prisca and Aquila (Rom. 16:3-5)

Epaenetus, a Jewish-Christian formerly expelled from Rome, is bitter about having lost so much of his property and having to flee his city as a refugee. Now he is back but still has little. He is considering joining other returning Jews, including those in the synagogue, to protest oppressive taxes and the general discrimination against Jews in Rome. What can this house church do for Epaenetus?

For the Christian slaves working and living in the households of Aristobulus or Narcissus (Rom. 16:10-11)

Neither the house churches of the Saints (16:15) nor the Brothers and Sisters (16:14) can pay the high taxes that they owe the government. Some of them are considering joining in a tax revolt that includes other Jews from the synagogues, as well as foreigners who are pagans and too poor to pay what the government demands.

Would you consider helping either of these house churches financially if they asked you for help to pay their taxes? It may mean you will have to share some of the hard-earned cash you were saving to buy your freedom.

On the other hand, since you work for a master who is high up in the government, you do not want any Jew or Jewish-Christian to make political trouble. It may affect your house church and you might lose your status and perhaps be beaten, crucified, or at least sold away from Rome.

For those in the house churches of the brothers and sisters (Rom. 16:14) and the saints (Rom. 16:15)

Your house church is too poor to pay your taxes, but you know you will get into big trouble and lose your business if you do not pay. Some of the more militant Jews in your house-church want to join the tax revolt that includes other Jews from the synagogues as well as poor, foreign pagans living in Rome. But this will call attention to your house church and may make it illegal to meet as a church. You know the churches that meet in the households of Aristobulus and Narcissus are wealthier than you. Would you consider asking them for money?

1. If this letter is so tied to a specific historical situation, how much of it is still relevant today? How can we interpret other biblical writings in the context of our modern church communities?

2. Is the main thesis of Romans in 1:16-17 as relevant for us today as it was for first-century Christians? Why or why not? Is this thesis taken seriously in your own local congregation?

3. "I don't feel oppressed by the Law. It is my joy to obey and my security to help me live in a way that leads me to God." Is there a place for the Law in our lives and churches today?

4. Our society thinks in psychological and individualistic categories. Is it possible to think back into the minds of early Christians who did not understand concepts such as universal democracy, individual rights, or the power of the unconscious? Does the gospel take a different shape now than it did then? How might it be different? How might ethical implications be different?

5. Paul uses a good deal of slave imagery, since slavery was a fact of life in the Roman Empire. Is it appropriate or helpful to use slave imagery today?

6. How do we deal with diversity in our churches today? Differences in theology? Diversity on issues of race or class status, and on controversial topics like women's ordination, abortion, or homosexuality? How far can we tolerate differences in the spirit of Romans 14?

7. If Paul's discussion of one's attitude toward the state (13:1-7) reflects something of the political situation of his time, how do we interpret it for our lives today?

8. Much of what Paul says is shaped by his eschatology, his strong hope

of the eventual triumph of Jesus Christ over all the powers of evil and of God's renewal of all creation. Compare his hope with our hope for the future. The end of time has not yet come nearly 2,000 years later, and our scientific understanding has grown tremendously. Has this changed our expectations for the future?

9. Can Romans lend insight into how to relate to Jewish people or the nation of Israel? How?

10. Does the message get through? After one simulation on Romans 14:1–15:6, I received the following email from a first-year college student:

> Since I was not healthy enough to be in class, I have decided to write you an email from my room during the same time. The purpose of this email is not to talk of my not being at class. It is to tell you how the class as a whole has affected my life. I came from a Christian high school so a lot of the exegesis and hermeneutics are not new to me. However, this new development of the Roman House Church simulation has been very interesting.
>
> Just last night I had a very interesting, deep, and intellectual conversation with a girl concerning her opinion on homosexual marriage and abortion. I am good friends with this girl. I believe she is a good Christian who loves the Lord. But I terribly disagree with her opinions on the subjects. Before I came to college I might have dismissed her as a questionable Christian and definitely in need of some guidance in terms of biblical interpretation. Basically, I would, before college, have written her off as "one of those" Christians.
>
> All that to say that, as I was talking with her last night, I realized mid-conversation that this is exactly what the Roman House Churches were doing 2000 years ago. Christians, true Christians, were debating controversial issues. Yet God, through Paul, demands unity. So despite my contrary beliefs, we still need to strive for unity, and I need to respect her. This is something I have struggled with in the past when people have disagreed with me in relation to scriptural interpretation.
>
> This is why it matters:
>
> I have always applied Paul's teaching on unity in a different way: to

love your Christian brother [or sister]. My problem was, due to certain beliefs, I would doubt another's true conversion. At that point, they are no longer part of the Body and I don't have to be one with them. This study has shown me that for 2,000 years Christians have disagreed with each other, but agreeing to disagree in many cases considering salvation does not stand or fall on many of the topics.

Just wanted to let you know your class is having an effect on my life.

KAI KASIGURAN

If you are a visitor to the class studying Romans, read this page first. We are in the midst of a series of lessons on Paul's letter to the Roman Christians. We are listening to the text as much as possible as Paul's original audience would have heard it.

To do this, we are simulating the five Roman house churches which probably existed at the time Paul wrote in A.D. 57 or 58. Each member of the class role-plays a character in one of these house churches. Some of the characters, however, do not yet feel accepted in the house church which they attend. They are Jewish refugees who were expelled from Rome eight or nine years earlier by the emperor Claudius. But now Nero is emperor, and he is more favorable to Jews, so they have been allowed to return.

These Jewish refugees want to return to the church groups they left, but many things have changed. Instead of meeting in synagogues, they meet in homes. Gentiles have taken over leadership, and the Law is not being kept as carefully as before. The Scriptures are not read as carefully anymore. The worship liturgy is more charismatic, perhaps colored by the religious backgrounds of the Gentile Christians. The refugees are critical of the house churches they used to belong to, but they need them for economic as well as spiritual reasons. Should the house churches accept these Jewish refugees back into membership?

Paul is concerned about the factions in the Roman churches, about the conservatives who condemn others, and the liberals who despise those who have scruples. He wants to bring everyone together in unity, even though lifestyles are different. Paul is especially concerned about the Roman churches because he needs their support. He is leaving to take the collection from the Gentiles to the poor Jewish Christians in Jerusalem, and then he wants to visit Rome and gather support and expertise for his mission to preach the gospel in Spain. He wants everyone to get along with each other in peace and harmony for the sake of his mission.

Paul's letter, therefore, is a brilliantly constructed ambassadorial letter of good will to all factions in Rome. It insists on only one way to God — through faith in Jesus Christ, and not through either the Law or freedom from the Law. It is meant to be proclaimed to all the churches, most likely by Phoebe, who carried it there. Phoebe is Paul's patron, who is probably helping fund his mission to Spain. She is also a deacon and leader in the church at Cenchreae, near Corinth.

During the class hour we meet in house-church groupings. "Phoebe" reads the appropriate text, and the house churches discuss what they've heard and how they feel about it in their particular role as Jew or Gentile, rich or poor, slave or free.

Bibliography

Aune, David E. "Romans as a *Logos Protreptikos*." In *The Romans Debate*, edited by Karl P. Donfried, 278-96. Peabody, Mass.: Hendrickson, 1991.

Balch, David L., ed. *Homosexuality, Science, and the "Plain Sense" of Scripture.* Grand Rapids: Eerdmans, 2000.

Banks, Robert. *Paul's Idea of Community: The Early House Churches in Their Historical Setting.* Grand Rapids: Eerdmans, 1980.

Bornkamm, Günther. "The Letter to the Romans as Paul's Last Will and Testament." In *The Romans Debate*, edited by Karl P. Donfried, 16-28. Peabody, Mass.: Hendrickson, 1991.

Bowers, W. P. "Jewish Communities in Spain in the Time of Paul the Apostle." *Journal of Theological Studies* 26 (1975): 395-402.

Bradley, Keith R. "On the Roman Slave Supply and Slavebreeding." In *Classical Slavery*, edited by M. I. Finley, 42-64. London: Frank Cass & Co., 1987.

———. *Slaves and Masters in the Roman Empire: A Study in Social Control.* Collection Latomus, vol. 185. Bruxelles: Revue d'études Latines, 1984.

Branick, Vincent. *The House Church in the Writings of Paul.* Wilmington: Michael Glazier, 1989.

Briggs, Sheila. "Sexual Justice and the Righteousness of God." In *Sex and God*, edited by Linda Hurcombe. New York: Routledge & Kegan Paul, 1987.

Burford, Alison. *Craftsmen in Greek and Roman Society.* London: Thames and London, 1972.

Burkert, Walter. *Ancient Mystery Cults.* Cambridge, Mass.: Harvard University Press, 1987.

Campbell, William S. *Paul's Gospel in an Intercultural Context.* New York: Peter Lang, 1991.

Carcopino, Jerome. *Daily Life in Ancient Rome: The People and the City at the Height of the Empire.* Trans. Henry T. Rowell. New Haven: Yale University Press, 1940.

Cary, M., and H. H. Scullard. *A History of Rome Down to the Reign of Constantine.* London: Macmillan, 1975.

Charlesworth, James H., ed. *The Old Testament Pseudepigrapha.* Vol. 2. New York: Doubleday, 1985.

Cranfield, C. E. B. *The Epistle to the Romans.* Edinburgh: T. & T. Clark, 1979.

Cutler, Daniel S. *The Bible Cookbook: Lore of Food in Biblical Times Plus Modern Adaptations of Ancient Recipes.* New York: Wm. Morrow & Co., 1985.

Danker, Frederick. *Benefactor.* Chicago: Clayton Publishing House, 1982.

Donfried, Karl P., ed. *The Romans Debate* (revised and expanded). Peabody, Mass.: Hendrickson, 1991.

Dunn, James D. G. *Word Biblical Commentary,* vol. 38A: *Romans 1–8,* vol. 38B: *Romans 9–16.* Waco, Tex.: Word Books, 1988.

Ellis, E. Earle. *Paul's Use of the Old Testament.* Edinburgh: Oliver and Boyd, 1957.

Ferguson, Everett. *Backgrounds of Early Christianity.* Grand Rapids: Eerdmans, 1987.

Ferguson, John. *The Religions of the Roman Empire.* Ithaca, N.Y.: Cornell University Press, 1970.

Finger, Thomas N. *Christian Theology: An Eschatological Approach.* 2 vols. Scottdale, Pa.: Herald Press, 1985-89.

Fiorenza, Elisabeth Schüssler. *Bread Not Stone: The Challenge of Feminist Biblical Interpretation.* Boston: Beacon, 1984.

————, ed. *In Memory of Her: A Feminist Theological Reconstruction of Christian Origins.* New York: Crossroad, 1983.

Freedman, D. N., ed. *The Anchor Bible Dictionary.* 6 vols. New York: Doubleday, 1992.

Frier, Bruce W. *Landlords and Tenants in Imperial Rome.* Princeton: Princeton University Press, 1980.

Gamble, Harry, Jr. *A Textual History of the Letter to the Romans.* Studies and Documents, vol. 42. Grand Rapids: Eerdmans, 1977.

Grant, Frederick C. *Hellenistic Religions.* Normal, Ala.: Liberal Arts Press, 1953.

Hartmann, Lars. "Baptism." In *The Anchor Bible Dictionary,* edited by D. N. Freedman. New York: Doubleday, 1992.

Hays, Richard B. *Echoes of Scripture in the Letters of Paul.* New Haven: Yale University Press, 1989.

Hengel, Martin. *Victory over Violence: Jesus and the Revolutionaries.* Philadelphia: Fortress, 1973.

Jerusalem Bible, The. New York: Doubleday, 1966.

Jewett, Robert. *Christian Tolerance: Paul's Message to the Modern Church.* Philadelphia: Westminster, 1982.

—————. "Following the Argument of Romans." *Word and World* 6, no. 4 (1986): 382-89.

—————. "The Law and the Coexistence of Jews and Gentiles in Romans." *Interpretation* 39, no. 4 (Oct. 1985): 341-56.

—————. "Paul, Phoebe, and the Spanish Mission." In *The Social World of Formative Christianity and Judaism,* edited by Jacob Neusner et al. Philadelphia: Fortress, 1988.

—————. *Romans.* Cokesbury Basic Bible Commentary. Nashville: Graded Press, 1987.

—————. *Romans: A Commentary.* Hermeneia. Minneapolis: Augsburg Fortress, 2006.

—————. "Romans as an Ambassadorial Letter." *Interpretation* 36, no. 1 (Jan. 1982): 5-20.

—————. "The Social Context and Implications of Homoerotic References in Romans." In *Homosexuality, Science, and the "Plain Sense" of Scripture,* edited by David L. Balch. Grand Rapids: Eerdmans, 2000.

—————. "To All of God's Beloved in Rome: A Cross-Cultural Analysis of the Recipients of Paul's Letter." Unpublished lecture, March 24, 1988.

Josephus, Flavius. *Antiquities of the Jews.*

Joshel, Sandra R. *Work, Identity, and Legal Status at Rome: A Study of the Occupational Inscriptions.* Oklahoma Series in Classical Culture. Norman and London: University of Oklahoma Press, 1992.

Juvenal. *Satires.*

Karris, Robert J. "Romans 14:1–15:13 and the Occasion of Romans." In *The Romans Debate,* edited by Karl P. Donfried. Peabody, Mass.: Hendrickson, 1991.

Kee, Howard Clark. *Christian Origins in Sociological Perspective.* Philadelphia: Westminster, 1980.

Kennedy, George. *New Testament Interpretation Through Rhetorical Criticism.* Chapel Hill and London: University of North Carolina Press, 1984.

Kraemer, Ross Shepard. *Her Share of the Blessings: Women's Religions Among Pagans, Jews, and Christians in the Greco-Roman World.* New York: Oxford University Press, 1992.

Lampe, Peter. *Die stadtrömischen Christen in den ersten beiden Jahrhunderten: Untersuchen zur Sozialgeschichte.* Tübingen: J. C. B. Mohr, 1989. E.T.: *From Paul to Valentinus: Christians at Rome in the first two centuries.* Trans. Michael Steinhauser. Minneapolis: Fortress, 2003.

————. "The Roman Christians of Romans 16." In *The Romans Debate*, edited by Karl P. Donfried, 216-30. Peabody, Mass.: Hendrickson, 1991.

Leon, Harry J. *The Jews of Ancient Rome*. The Morris Loeb Series. Philadelphia: Jewish Publication Society of America, 1960.

Lightfoot, J. B. *St. Paul's Epistle to the Philippians*. London and Cambridge: Macmillan, 1873.

Longacre, Doris Janzen. *More-with-Less Cookbook*. Scottdale, Pa.: Herald Press, 1976.

Mack, Burton L. *Rhetoric and the New Testament*. Minneapolis: Fortress, 1990.

MacMullen, Ramsay. *Roman Social Relations: 50 B.C. to A.D. 284*. New Haven: Yale University Press, 1974.

————. "Tax-Pressure in the Roman Empire." *Latomus* 46 (1987): 737.

Malherbe, Abraham J. *Social Aspects of Early Christianity*. Philadelphia: Fortress, 1983.

McGinn, Sheila E. *Celebrating Romans: Template for Pauline Theology*. Grand Rapids: Eerdmans, 2004.

McKibbin, Jean and Frank. *Cookbook of Foods from Bible Days*. Culver City: Franje, 1971.

Meeks, Wayne A. *The First Urban Christians: The Social World of the Apostle Paul*. New Haven: Yale University Press, 1983.

Minear, Paul. *The Obedience of Faith*. Naperville, Ill.: Alec R. Allenson, 1971.

Murphy-O'Connor, Jerome. *St. Paul's Corinth: Texts and Archaeology*. Wilmington: Michael Glazier, 1989.

Osiek, Carolyn, RSCJ. *What Are They Saying About the Social Setting of the New Testament?* Mahwah, N.J.: Paulist Press, 1984.

Pomeroy, Sarah B. *Goddesses, Whores, Wives, and Slaves: Women in Classical Antiquity*. New York: Schocken Books, 1975.

Reasoner, Mark. "The 'Strong' and the 'Weak' in Rome and in Paul's Theology." Unpublished Ph.D. dissertation. University of Chicago, 1990. Published as: *The Strong and the Weak: Romans 14:1–15:13 in Context*. Society for New Testament Monograph Series. Cambridge: Cambridge University Press, 1999.

Rhoads, David M. *Israel in Revolution 6-74 C.E.: A Political History Based on the Writings of Josephus*. Philadelphia: Fortress 1976.

Riekkinen, Vilho. *Römer 13: Aufzeichnung und Weiterführung der exegetischen Aussprache* (Romans 13: Description and advancement of the exegetical discussion). Helsinki: Suomalainen Tiedekatemia, 1980.

Rose, H. S. *Religion in Greece and Rome*. New York: Harper & Row, 1959.

Saller, Richard P. *Personal Patronage Under the Early Empire.* Cambridge: Cambridge University Press, 1982.

———. "Slavery and the Roman Family." In *Classical Slavery,* edited by M. I. Finley, 65-87. London: Frank Cass & Co., 1987.

Sanday, W., and A. C. Headlam. *The Epistle to the Romans.* The International Critical Commentary. New York: Charles Scribner, 1915.

Stambaugh, John E., and David L. Balch. *The New Testament in Its Social Environment.* Philadelphia: Westminster Press, 1986.

Stirewalt, Martin Luther, Jr. "The Form and Function of the Greek Letter-Essay." In *The Romans Debate,* edited by Karl P. Donfried, 147-71. Peabody, Mass.: Hendrickson, 1991.

Tacitus. *Annals.*

Thiessen, Gerd. *The Social Setting of Pauline Christianity.* Philadelphia: Fortress, 1982.

Tidball, Derek. *The Social Context of the New Testament: A Sociological Analysis.* Grand Rapids: Zondervan, 1984.

Toews, John E. *Romans.* Believers Bible Commentary. Scottdale, Pa.; Waterloo, Ont.: Herald Press, 2004.

Watson, N. W. "The Interpretation of Romans VII." *Australian Biblical Review* 21 (1973): 27-39.

Wiedemann, Thomas. *Greek and Roman Slavery.* Baltimore: Johns Hopkins University Press, 1981.

Wiefel, Wolfgang. "The Jewish Community in Ancient Rome and the Origins of Roman Christianity." In *The Romans Debate,* edited by Karl P. Donfried, 85-101. Peabody, Mass.: Hendrickson, 1991.

Wink, Walter. *Engaging the Powers: Discernment and Resistance in a World of Domination.* Minneapolis: Fortress, 1992.

———. *Naming the Powers: The Language of Power in the New Testament.* Philadelphia: Fortress, 1984.

———. *Unmasking the Powers: The Invisible Forces That Determine Human Existence.* Philadelphia: Fortress, 1986.

Winter, Bruce W. "The Public Honouring of Christian Benefactors: Romans 13:3-4 and 1 Peter 2:14-15." *Journal for the Study of the New Testament* 34 (1988): 87-90.

Wuellner, Wilhelm. "Paul's Rhetoric of Argumentation in Romans." In *The Romans Debate,* edited by Karl P. Donfried. Peabody, Mass.: Hendrickson, 1991.

Index